Instant Pot

An Ultimate Guide to the New Pressure Cooker

200 Fast, Healthy and Delicious Recipes

Table of Contents

MAIN COURSE RECIPES

SOUPS

Introduction

The Instant Pot Pressure Cooker is a handy kitchen gadget with 7 different functions. This means that you have the convenience of a rice cooker, a slow cooker, a browning/sauté pan, a pressure cooker, a yogurt maker, a steamer, and a warming pot. All of these functions are performed in one pot! You may not be able to store and use all of those appliances in your kitchen, so the instant pot is a great solution.

This book has been split into two sections. The first will tell you all that you need to know about the Instant Pot, including its history, how to use and clean it, and what to do if problems arise. In the second section, you will find taste bud, tantalizing recipes to try out in your cooker.

What are you waiting for? Start with the background so you know how to use your Instant Pot and then check out the recipes. You may find that it becomes your favorite cooking gadget after the first few times you use it.

SECTION I

About the Instant Pot

The Instant Pot Pressure Cooker has a multitude of functions. The sleek, high-tech design has conveniently labeled buttons on the front that work as a browning/sauté pan, warmer, slow cooker, yogurt maker, rice cooker, steamer, and of course, pressure cooker. This chapter will teach you all that you need to know about the instant pot, from the history of its design to how to troubleshoot common issues.

The History of the Instant Pot

The instant pot starts with a pressure cooker. A French physicist named Denis Papin invented the pressure cooker in 1679. The original pressure cooker was a sealed cooking vessel, generally used on the stove top. It does not allow steam to escape unless it reaches a certain temperature and since higher levels or pressure raise the boiling temperature of water, it takes longer for water to turn into a steam. This allows food to be cooked more rapidly and also infuses it with steam, resulting in the flavor, juiciness, and tenderness that you get from slow cooking meats.

The pressure cooker first became popular during World War II. Since it allowed cheaper cuts of meat to be cooked in less time, it became highly popular as a means to save energy and money on groceries.

Historians are not sure who is responsible for the electric pressure cooker, which mimicked the stovetop pressure cooker but without the stovetop. Many credit the man who filed the first patent for the electric pressure cooker on January 9, 1991- a Chinese scientist named Yong-Guang Wang.

The electric pressure cooker consists of several parts that work together to simulate the stovetop cooking process used during World War II. Over time, engineers wondered about a pressure cooker that could do more, based on the program it was set on. This is how programmable multi-function cookers, like the Instant Pot, came to be. Meeting the demand for different ways to cook food in limited space lead to the Instant Pot. After all, storing all 7 appliances that you get with the Instant Pot would take up quite a bit of room. After just a few years on the market, it has plenty of fans and is gaining an even greater fan base as more people hear about it.

How to Use the Control Panel and Automatic Cooking Programs

The great thing about the Instant Pot is that it has an easy-to-understand control panel- once you know what you are doing. Here are the buttons you will find on the pot, as well as how to use and adjust each one.

♦ **Manual Buttons**- The manual button allows you to use the Instant Pot without any of the pre-set functions. Since a lot of the recipes you will find are for use in all types of multi-function pots, you may find that you use these quite often when reading from a recipe. The manual button allows you to cook on high pressure for a set number of minutes. You will use the + and – buttons to adjust the cooking time.

♦ **Cancel/Keep Warm**- If you have pressed a function button and need to cancel it or turn of your pot, you use this button. You can also adjust the temperature to keep your food warm without cooking it. The average is 145 degrees, but you can use the + button to warm your food at 167 degrees or the – button to warm your food at 133 degrees

♦ **Brown/Sauté**- This button is useful for using your cooker with the lid off. Pressing sauté allows you to sauté in the pan. If you press the adjust button once, it will brown your food. If you press the adjust button twice, it will turn down the temperature and allow you to simmer.

♦ **Pressure**- The pressure button is used to switch between low and high pressure for the different types of cooking, though it does not work with all of the presets.

- **Timer-** This is a really handy button, especially if you want to throw everything in the pot in the morning and then have it automatically start cooking later in the day. Set the cooking function first and make any adjustments that you may need to. Then, press the timer button and use the + and − buttons to set the time.

- **Slow Cooker-** The default of this is a 4 hour cook time, but you can use the + and - buttons to adjust the time. You can also use the adjust button to set it for a low cooking temperature of 190-201 Fahrenheit, a normal cooking temperature of 194-205 Fahrenheit, or a high cooking temperature of 199-210 Fahrenheit.

- **Steam-** This is a high pressure preset that has a 10 minute cook time. You can adjust it to 15 minutes with the adjust button or 3 minutes by pressing the adjust button again. Since you don't want food to come in direct contact with the bottom of the pot, use this with a steamer basket or rack.

- **Yogurt-** As the button function name suggests, this setting is made for preparing yogurt. The preset is 8 hours long but you can adjust the time. You will find a recipe for this later. You control how tart the yogurt is by adjusting the time of the program- the longer time your yogurt spends in the cooker, the tarter it will be.

- **Rice-** The rice pre-set is made for white rice and the cooker will adjust itself based on the quantities of rice and water that are put in the pot. You may find that you prefer to cook the rice in less time by using high pressure though.

- **Porridge-** This is a high pressure setting with a default cook time of 20 minutes. You can adjust it to a higher 30 minute cook time or a lower 15 minute cook time.

- **Multi-grain-** This is a high pressure setting with a default cook time of 40 minutes. You can adjust it to a 20 minute cook time or a 60 minute cooking time. The

60 minute cook time also has a 45 minute soaking cycle before cooking.

- **Bean/Chili-** This high pressure cooking setting has a default of 30 minutes, though it can be adjusted to 40 minutes or 25 minutes.

- **Poultry-** Another high cooking pressure setting, this one with a 15 minute cook time. It can be adjusted to either 30 minutes or 5 minutes.

- **Soup-** This high pressure setting offers a default 30 minute cook time, being able to be adjusted for a 40 minute cook time or a 20 minute cook time by pressing the adjust button.

- **Meat/Stew-** This cooking setting preset is high pressure and defaults to 35 minutes. It can also be adjusted to 45 minutes or 20 minutes.

How to Clean the Instant Pot

For basic after-meal cleanup, you will want to clean the inner pot. You can remove this if that makes it easier. If you do get the outside of the inner pot wet though, be sure it is thoroughly dried before you put it back inside the housing unit. You should also wipe down the outer housing unit.

Sometimes, however, you will want to deep clean your Instant Pot to get rid of any leftover food and other residue that can cause odor. Built up residue can also cause the Instant Pot to malfunction, especially on the sealing ring and other areas that are essential to maintaining the pressure of the cooker.

Start by unplugging the pot, as you always should when cleaning electrical appliances to prevent electrocution. If it has recently been used, allow the Instant Pot to cool before cleaning. Then, gather everything you will need including a microfiber or cotton cloth, a small scrub brush, dish soap, and vinegar.

Take the lid and interior pot out of the Instant Pot and set to the side. Use a damp cloth to clean dried residue from the inside of the housing, being very cautions of getting water in any of the electrical components. If your lid needs a deep cleaning, remove the steam-release handle and wipe away any food particles. Then, remove the anti-block shield from under the lid and wipe the steam valve clean (DO NOT REMOVE THE STEAM VALVE).

Next, remove the sealing ring that holds the float valve in place, followed by the float valve itself. Clean both of these parts and be sure they are completely dry before reassembling the pot to prevent damage to your electrical components.

Then, remove the sealing ring. You will want to soak this in vinegar to remove any odors from food residue. Take the inner pot and clean it as you normally would, either by hand or in the dishwasher. You should also take the opportunity to clean the steam rack during this time. Finally, take vinegar and a cloth to remove any discoloration on the inner pot.

Once all of the parts are clean and dry, reassemble the pressure cooker. Make sure that you fit everything into position properly so your Instant Pot works the way it is supposed to.

How to Troubleshoot Common Problems

The good news is that the majority of problems that you have with the Instant Pot can be solved with a deep cleaning. Something you must be very caution of, however, is getting water in the housing unit, control panel, or other electrical parts. Water can cause your pot to short or malfunction, possibly even ruining it.

If cleaning the parts of your Instant Pot does not work, check to make sure all of the individual parts are in place properly. One area you should pay special attention to is the sealing ring. It must be sitting properly for the cooker to seal and create the high pressure it needs. Some other areas that are highly susceptible to cause your pot to function improperly because of food residue include the steam release handle, the float valve, and the anti-block shield.

If you deep clean the pot, be sure to check for signs of cracking, wear, or other malformation. You should also check the cord for damage. Contact the company to find out how to get replacement parts for the Instant Pot to get your cooker working like new again.

Well, there you have it. You now know all that you need to use, clean, and troubleshoot your Instant Pot, as well as interesting tidbits about its history. In the next section, you will find incredibly simple recipes to use in your Instant Pot.

SECTION II
Instant Pot Meals

Breakfast Recipes

Cranberry French Toast

If you are feeling the holiday season, this cranberry-packed pudding style breakfast is a great place to get into the spirit. The tart cranberries pair beautifully with a sweet orange sauce for a breakfast that your taste buds will thank you for.

Ingredients

For the French toast:

- 1 loaf Challah bread (cubed)
- 4 tablespoons butter (melted)
- 3 eggs (whisked together)
- 2 cups whole milk
- ½ cup sugar
- 1 teaspoon vanilla extract
- Zest of one orange (grated)
- ¼ teaspoon salt

For the sauce:

- ¼ cup fresh orange juice
- ½ cup sugar
- 2 cups fresh cranberries (rinsed)
- ¼ teaspoon cinnamon
- ¼ teaspoon salt

You will also need a baking dish small enough to fit in your pressure cooker, about 7" x 3" in size.

Instructions

Put everything for the sauce in a pot on the stove and bring to a boil using medium-high heat. Cook about 5 minutes, berries should start to pop. Grease your baking dish and add the sauce to it. Set this to the side.

Use a whisk to combine the sugar and melted butter for the French toast in a large bowl. Add all the rest of the ingredients (except the bread) and combine. Once combined, add the bread cubes and allow to rest until the bread absorbs the mixture, stirring occasionally for an even coating. Spread this on top of the cranberry orange sauce.

For easy removal of your dish, make a foil strip that is 36" long and fold it in half. Put a rack inside of your Instant Pot and add 1 cup of water. Layer your foil on the rack and then position the pan on top of that. Set to high pressure and let cook 25 minutes, then quick release pressure. If you would like the top to be browned, you may put it in the broiler for a few minutes.

♦ *6 servings*

Mushroom Thyme Oatmeal

If you are craving something savory for breakfast, this is an excellent choice. This recipe is an alternative to traditionally sweet oatmeal recipes and it is sure to hit the spot. It is reminiscent of risotto, so if you are a fan of that then you will be a fan of this savory breakfast oatmeal.

Ingredients

- 1 14-ounce can chicken broth
- 1 cup crimini mushrooms (sliced)
- 1 cup steel cut oats
- ¼ teaspoon salt
- 1 small onion (minced)
- Pepper to taste
- ½ cup smoked gouda (finely grated)
- ½ cup water
- 3 sprigs thyme (plus more for garnish if you would like)
- 2 garlic cloves (minced)
- 2 tablespoons olive oil

Instructions

Put the butter in the Instant Pot and put on the sauté setting. Once warmed, place in the onions. Let cook for 3 minutes. Mix in garlic and cook for another minute, until it becomes fragrant. Then, add the oats and continue to sauté for a minute. Put the thyme, broth, water, pepper and salt in the pressure cooker and set to high pressure for ten minutes.

While you are waiting, melt the oil in a pan over the stove using medium-high heat. Add the mushrooms and cook until well browned. Once the oats are done cooking, use a quick pressure release and stir them. Then, add the gouda and stir. Once melted, stir in the mushrooms and add salt and pepper if needed.

- *4 servings*

14

Scotch Eggs

Scotch eggs contain sausage and eggs, which are typically a breakfast food in the United States and the reason that this recipe was placed in this category. In the United Kingdom, it is not uncommon for this tasty meal to be served as lunch, alongside a pickle. This recipe is kept simple, with just 3 ingredients.

Ingredients

- 1 pound ground sausage (country style)
- 4 large eggs
- 1 tablespoon vegetable oil

Instructions

You are going to cook your eggs first. Start by placing the steamer basket inside the pressure cooker and a cup of water and your eggs. Cook for 6 minutes on high pressure. Use a natural release once the timer goes off for six minutes, then do a quick pressure release. Transfer the eggs to water so they can cool.

Once chilled, peel the eggs. Use ¼ pound of the sausage to encase each egg, making a sausage "meatball" around the egg. Turn the Instant Pot to its browning setting and add the oil. Use this to brown the Scotch eggs on all sides, turning as needed. Once browned, take the scotch eggs out of the pressure cooker and set aside.

Add 1 cup of water and a rack inside the pressure cooker. Put your scotch eggs on this rack and cook for 6 minutes on high pressure. Use a quick release when finished.

- *Serves 4*

Crustless Meat Lovers Quiche

This crustless egg dish is light and fluffy, as well as packed with all your favorite breakfast meats including sausage, bacon, and ham. It's also topped with cheese, because what egg breakfast would be complete without gooey cheese?

Ingredients

- 1 cup sausage (cooked)
- 2 green onions (chopped)
- 4 slices bacon (cooked and diced)
- ½ cup ham (diced)
- 1/8 teaspoon pepper
- 6 large eggs (whisked together)
- ½ cup milk
- 1 cup shredded cheese
- ¼ teaspoon salt

You will also need a 1 quart soufflé dish that will fit inside of your Instant Pot.

Instructions

Put a metal rack across the bottom of the Instant Pot. Add ½ cup of water. Then, combine the eggs, milk, salt, and pepper in a bowl. Set this to the side and layer your meats, green onions, and cheese across the bottom of the pan. Pour the eggs over this and stir gently to combine.

Cover with foil, being sure not to cover it completely. To make it easier to remove your soufflé dish, create a 36" of aluminum foil and fold it in half. Layer this under the soufflé dish ad set your soufflé dish on top of the rack.

Cook on high pressure for 30 minutes. Once the soufflé is done cooking, allow it to sit for 10 minutes and then do a quick pressure release. Remove the dish and take the foil off the top. If you choose, you can also sprinkle some extra cheese on the top and place it in the broiler. This won't add much to the flavor, but it does a lot for the presentation. For best results, serve your quiche immediately.

- *4 servings*

Apple Cherry Risotto

Risotto is rather versatile. It can be paired with sweet or savory flavors to make something delicious, which makes it perfect for this breakfast recipe. Sweet apple, tart cherry, and creamy risotto come together beautifully in this breakfast dish.

Ingredients

- 1 ½ cups Arborio rice
- 1 cup apple juice
- ½ cup dried cherries
- 2 large apples (peel, core, and dice)
- 3 cups milk
- 2 tablespoons butter
- 1 ½ teaspoons cinnamon
- 1/3 cup brown sugar

Instructions

Place butter in the pressure cooker and simmer for two to three minutes. Then, add the rice, stirring until the rice becomes opaque. This should take 3-4 minutes. Then, mix in the brown sugar, apples, and spices; stir to combine. Add the milk and juice and stir. Then, cook for 6 minutes on high pressure.

Use a quick pressure release once the risotto is done. Stir in the dried cherries. If you choose, you can top with a splash of milk, slice almonds, or extra brown sugar.

♦ *4 servings*

Bacon, Egg Casserole

This savory breakfast makes great use of the slow cook setting. You can easily manipulate the flavors in the recipe by changing out the fillings.

Ingredients

- cooking spray
- ¼ tsp pepper
- ½ tsp salt
- ½ c milk
- 12 eggs
- 6 green onions, sliced
- 8 oz cheddar cheese
- 8 slices bacon, cooked and chopped
- 20 oz bag hash browns

Instructions

Grease the pot with nonstick spray. Put half of you hash brown on the bottom. Then layer with half of the bacon and cheese, and the 1/3 of the onion. Repeat with remaining hash brown, then bacon, then cheese, and another third of the onion.

Whisk the pepper, salt, milk, and eggs together in a bowl. Pour over the hash brown layers. Set to slow cook. Set to low for four to five hours, or two to three hours on high. Serve with extra onions.

- *8 servings*

French Toast Casserole

This sweet breakfast will be a favorite for everyone. You will be fixing every morning when you get the taste of all the delicious flavors

Ingredients

- ½ tsp cinnamon
- 1/3 c diced pecans
- 2 egg whites
- 1 tsp lemon juice
- 3 tbsp honey
- 3 c diced apple pieces
- 9 slices bread
- 1 tsp vanilla
- 2 eggs
- ½ tsp cinnamon
- 2 tbsp honey
- 1 ½ c milk

Instructions

Mix the last 6 ingredients together in a bowl. Spray your cooker with cooking spray. Toss the first 5 ingredients together and set aside. Slice the bread in triangles. Place a single layer of bread in the bottom. Top with ¼ of your apple mixture. Continue doing this until you have used all of your bread and top with the rest of the apple mixture. Pour eggs over the bread. Set to slow cook, and set for two and a half hours on high, or four hours on low. The bread should have time to absorb all of the liquid. Serve with a drizzle of maple syrup.

- 12 servings

Greek Egg Casserole

These eggs have lots extra veggies added in. They can also be traded for your favorite veggies of choice.

Ingredients

- ½ c feta cheese
- 1 tsp pepper
- ½ c sun dried tomatoes
- 2 c spinach
- ½ c milk
- 1 c sliced mushrooms
- ½ tsp salt
- 1 tbsp onion powder
- 1 tsp garlic powder
- 12 eggs, whisked

Instructions

Mix together the pepper, salt, milk, and eggs. Whisk in the garlic and onion powder. Stir in the spinach, mushrooms, and tomatoes. Pour this into you cooker. Sprinkle over the feta. Set to slow cook for 4-6 hours on low.

♦ *10 servings*

Quinoa Energy Bar

These are a time saver when you're in a hurry. After you take the time to fix them, they will be there for you to grab up.

Ingredients

- 2 tbsp chia seeds
- 1/3 c dried apples, chopped
- ½ c raisins
- 1/3 c quinoa
- ½ tsp cinnamon
- salt
- 1 c vanilla almond milk
- 2 tbsp almond butter
- 1/3 c toasted almonds, chopped
- 2 eggs
- 2 tbsp maple syrup

Instructions

Spray your cooker with nonstick spray and place parchment paper in the bottom. Spray again. In a heat proof bowl, combine the syrup and almond butter. Microwave in 20 second increments to make creamy. Mix in the salt, milk, and cinnamon. Mix until it is complete incorporated. Mix in eggs, and stir in all the rest of the ingredients. Pour into the cooker. Set to slow cook for 4 hours on low heat. Slide a knife along the edges and ease out bars. Set in the fridge to cool. Once cooled, cut into individual bars.

- *8 servings*

Sausage & Pepper Hash

This breakfast has lots of flavors, and has all the nutrients you need all in one pot.

Ingredients

- ♦ 2 tsp fresh tarragon
- ♦ ½ c swiss cheese
- ♦ 1 ½ c chopped red sweet peppers
- ♦ ¼ c chicken broth
- ♦ ½ tsp pepper
- ♦ ½ tsp thyme
- ♦ 1 ½ lbs red potatoes
- ♦ cooking spray
- ♦ 1 ½ c onion, sliced
- ♦ 1 tsp olive oil
- ♦ 12 oz package smoked sausage, sliced

Instructions

Coat your cooker with nonstick spray. Mix together pepper, thyme, potatoes, onion, and sausage. Pour in the broth. Set to slow cook. Set to low for five to six hours. Mix in the peppers and cheese. Serve with sprinkle of tarragon.

♦ *10 servings*

Breakfast Quinoa

Quinoa is easy to make in the pressure cooker and comes out perfect every time with this recipe. Quinoa retains its fluffy texture and reheats well, so you can make all 6 servings and refrigerate for another morning. Top with berries and slice almonds if you want an extra burst of flavor (and nutrition).

Ingredients

- 2 ¼ cups water
- ¼ teaspoon ground cinnamon
- 1 ½ cups quinoa (rinse well)
- 2 tablespoons maple syrup
- 1/8 teaspoon salt
- ½ teaspoon vanilla

Instructions

Add all of the ingredients to the Instant Pot and mix to combine. Cook for a minute of high pressure. Once finished, allow the quinoa to sit for 10 minutes before using a quick release. Use a fork to fluff the quinoa and serve with a splash of milk and your desired toppings.

- *6 servings*

Hard Boiled Egg

Boiled eggs are popular for breakfast, lunch and a snack. It's a no brainer to boil eggs in the Instant Pot. Fix as many as you want and refrigerate the rest for later.

Ingredients

- eggs, the amount you want
- 1 cup water

Instructions

Add the water into your pot, and carefully place the eggs in your steamer basket.

Close the lid and seal. Set for 5 minutes on manual. Once finished, let the pressure release for 5 minutes before using quick release.

Place the cooked eggs in cold water and then peel.

- *Servings varied*

Fruit Yogurt

Yogurt is a great option for a healthy breakfast. It also refrigerates well. This is an easy recipe to switch up. If you're not in the mood for fruit, mix in whatever add in you would like.

Ingredients

- 4 tbsp sugar
- 2 cup fruit, chopped
- 5 1/3 cup milk
- 4 tbsp milk powder
- 4 pint jars

Instructions

Place 1 ½ cups of water into you Instant pot and add a grate.

Place 1 1/3 cup milk in each jar and loosely top with lid. Place the jars in the pot. Set to yogurt for 2 minutes. Let the pressure release and carefully take out jars. Allow them to cool.

Mix in yogurt culture, 1 tbsp sugar, and 1 tbsp milk powder into each jar. Stir in a ½ cup of fruit into the jars. Place the lid on the jars and put into the pot. Set to yogurt for 12 hours. Refrigerate any leftovers.

♦ *4 servings*

Applesauce

Applesauce is a great thing to have on hand, especially if you have children. In works great for breakfast or a snack, and it keeps well too.

Ingredients

- 6 apples, peeled and cored
- ¼ tsp salt
- 1 tbsp lemon juice
- ½ cup water

Instructions

Mix everything in the Instant Pot. Close lid and seal. Set to high for 4 hours. Puree the cooked apples and add in cinnamon for flavor. This can be stored in an air tight bowl.

- *12 servings*

Egg Muffin

This is a quick breakfast that anybody will love. With bacon and onion, there is no shortage of flavor.

Ingredients

- ♦ 4 eggs
- ♦ 4 slice bacon, crumbled
- ♦ ½ tsp lemon pepper seasoning
- ♦ diced onion
- ♦ shredded cheese

Instructions

Pour 1 ½ cups of water into the pot and add in the steamer basket.

Mix together the seasoning and the eggs. Place equal amounts of cheese, onion, and bacon in 4 silicon cups. Fill each cup with egg mixture. Place the cups in the pot. Cover with lid and seal. Set to high for 8 minutes. Let them sit for 2 minutes before using quick release.

♦ *4 servings*

Meat Lover Quiche

This recipe allows you to have pizza for breakfast. It's not quite a pizza, but it gives you everything meat lover's love mixed into their eggs. You can easily add in extras of your choice

Ingredients

- 6 beaten eggs
- 1 cup cheese
- ½ cup milk
- onion, chopped
- salt
- ½ cup ham, diced
- pepper
- 1 cup sausage, cooked and crumbled
- 4 bacon slices, cooked and crumbled

Instructions

Pour 1 ½ cups water in the pot and add the trivet.

Combine everything and place into a heat safe soufflé dish. Loosely place foil over top of the dish. Using a foil sling, ease the dish into the pot. Cover with lid and seal. Set to high for thirty minutes. Allow to sit for ten minutes and the use quick release. Ease the dish out and top with extra cheese if desired.

♦ *6 servings*

Breakfast Hash

This is a fun breakfast full of nutrients to get you going. It can be easily modified to anyone's taste. It's also a quick way to fix a potato hash.

Ingredients

- large potato, diced
- 2 tsp paprika
- large sweet potato, diced
- ½ cup water
- 1 tsp salt
- 2 tsp cumin
- 2 garlic cloves, minced
- cayenne, to taste
- 2tbsp oil
- 2 cup bell pepper, chopped
- 1 tsp pepper

Instructions

Mix the vegetables in the oil and spices. Put the veggies in the pot and pour in a half cup of water. Seal the lid. Set to high for 10 minutes. Quick release pressure when finished.

Set to sauté and let it brown.

♦ *4 servings*

Pear Oatmeal

This is a great, protein filled, breakfast anybody would love. The added fruits, nuts and sugars can easily be modified to your own taste

Ingredients

- 2 cup milk
- ½ cup walnuts
- 1 tbsp butter, melted
- ½ cup raisins
- salt
- 2 cup pear, diced
- 4 tbsp brown sugar
- ½ tsp cinnamon
- 1 cup rolled oats

Instructions

Mix everything together in a heat safe bowl. Pour a cup of water in the pot and add in the trivet. Place the bowl into the pot and seal lid in place. Set for 6 minutes. Once finished, quick release the pressure.

- *4 servings*

MAIN COURSE RECIPES

Chicken Enchilada Pasta

With the pressure cooker, you can cook your pasta and your chicken in the same step, making dinner super easy to cook. This is packed full of flavor and tastes great topped with sour cream, salsa, jalapenos, green onions, diced tomatoes, or cilantro.

Ingredients

- 3 cups rotini pasta
- 1 cup onion (diced)
- 1 ¼ cup water
- 1 packet taco seasoning
- 1 10-ounce can Rotel tomatoes
- 2 boneless skinless chicken breasts (diced)
- 1 19-ounce can enchilada sauce
- 2 garlic cloves (diced)
- 2 cups shredded Mexican cheese

Instructions

Set your Instant Pot to the sauté setting and add the oil. Once hot, put the onion in and cook about 5 minutes. Mix in garlic, cook about 1 minute. Then, add the water, tomatoes, enchilada sauce, and taco seasoning to the pot and stir. Add the pasta and chicken breast.

Set on high pressure and cook for 4 minutes, using a quick pressure release when it is done. Continue to cook on sauté for an additional minute, until the pasta is tender. Pour the pasta into a baking dish and sprinkle with the Mexican cheese. Toss in the broiler until brown and crispy. Top with your choice of toppings before serving.

- *6 servings*

Chicken with Squash and Sweet Potato

This is a healthy one pot dish. The squash and potato adds a sweetness and texture to the dish that you can't get anywhere else.

Ingredients

- pepper
- 3tbsp basil
- 1 tsp minced garlic
- ½ c chicken broth
- salt
- 3 c butternut squash, peeled and chunked
- ½ lb chicken
- 3 tbsp parsley
- ¾ c sweet potato, peeled and diced

Instructions

Combine everything in the pot. Seal the lid. Set to poultry and cook for 9 minutes. Quick release pressure.

- *2 servings*

Corned Beef and Cabbage

One of the most popular Irish dishes just got easier. This is full of flavor and tender. A tasty dish that everyone will love, and it's perfect for St. Patrick's Day

Ingredients

- small head cabbage, wedges
- 1 medium carrots, chunked
- ½ lb potatoes
- ½ tsp thyme
- ¼ tsp whole allspice
- 2 whole peppercorns
- 1 bay leaf
- 2 garlic cloves, smashed
- ½ small onion
- 2 c water
- 2 lb corned beef brisket

Instructions

Put thyme, allspice, peppercorns, garlic cloves, onion, water, and brisket in the pot. Lock and seal lid and cook for 90 minutes. Turn off and naturally release pressure. Remove meat and tent with foil. Add cabbage, potatoes, and carrots to pot. Lock and seal lid. Let cook 10 minutes. Carefully let pressure release. Remove vegetables and serve with beef.

- *4 servings*

Chicken Parmigiana

This tasty Italian chicken dish is perfect served over your favorite pasta. It's full of flavor and easy to make.

Ingredients

- 4 c mozzarella cheese
- 48 oz tomato sauce
- 4tbsp butter
- ½ tsp garlic powder
- 1 c parmesan cheese
- 3 lb chicken tenders
- 1 c olive oil

Instructions

Set to sauté and heat the oil. Brown the chicken on all sides. Pour tomato sauce, butter, garlic, and parmesan on to the chicken. Seal lid. Set to poultry and cook 15 minutes, and then use quick release. Top with mozzarella cheese. Place lid on pot and allow the cheese to melt.

♦ *6 servings*

Italian Beef

This dish is full of flavor. With the tomatoes and vinegar, you get a nice tartness that helps to tenderize the beef.

Ingredients

- 1 bay leaf
- pepper
- salt
- ¼ tsp pickling salt
- 2 garlic cloves
- ¼ tsp minced garlic
- 1 tsp beef bouillon
- 2 tbsp water
- 1 ½ tsp wine vinegar
- 8 oz whole canned tomatoes
- 1 ½ lb beef roast

Instructions

Trim fat off of the meat, and cut to fit in the pot. Place the rest of the ingredients over meat. Seal lid. Set to meat/stew for 35 minutes. Carefully release pressure. Remove bay leaf.

♦ *2 servings*

Salmon

This a delicious, flavorful fish dish that couldn't be easier to make. It allows you to flavor the salmon any way you see fit.

Ingredients

- 1 c water, or liquid of choice
- 1 lb salmon, skin on
- sliced onion
- your choice of spices
- pepper
- sliced lemon
- salt

Instructions

Cut salmon in serving pieces. Sprinkle with pepper, salt and spices of your choice. Massage into the salmon. Line the pot with parchment paper or foil. Layer the aromatics in the pot. Lay salmon on top. Pour in your choice of liquid. It should almost cover the fish. Cook on low, 1 hour. It will vary depending on the salmon size. Carefully remove salmon by lifting up parchment or foil.

- *servings varied*

Chicken with Homemade Marinara Sauce and Mozzarella

This tasty recipe is like chicken Parmesan but lighter on the carbs since the chicken is not breaded. It tastes great over noodles or can be served with a side of bread. If you don't want to do the work to make the homemade marinara sauce, you can always substitute it with store bought.

Ingredients

- 1 14-ounce can crushed tomatoes in puree
- 1 cup water
- 1 teaspoon dried basil
- 4 boneless skinless chicken breasts
- 2 garlic cloves (crushed)
- ¼ teaspoon black pepper
- 1 tablespoon olive oil
- 1 cup low-fat Mozzarella cheese (grated)
- ¼ teaspoon salt
- ¼ teaspoon red pepper flakes

Instructions

Sprinkle the chicken with pepper and salt. Put the oil in the pot and set to the Browning setting. Brown the chicken breasts in two separate batches, setting the first on a plate while you are browning the second.

Once the chicken breast is all to the side, add oil to the pan if you do not have any left. Add the garlic and sauté until fragrant, about 1 minute. Add all of the ingredients except the mozzarella cheese to the Instant Pot and stir well to combine. Add the chicken breasts and cook five minutes on high, using a quick pressure release when it is finished.

Then, heat your broiler and prepare a casserole dish by coating it with a non-stick spray. Layer the chicken inside. Then, use the sauté function to simmer the sauce until it is as thick as you would like this. Cover the chicken and then top with mozzarella cheese. Put in the broiler until the cheese browns and enjoy.

- *4 servings*

Coq au Vin

This traditional French recipe is adapted to the pressure cooker so you can have a delicious meal in no time at all. Usually made in a slow cooker, this flavor-packed French chicken stew can easily be made for dinner without much planning.

Ingredients

- 3 pounds boneless skinless chicken
- ½ cup bacon (diced)
- 1 cup chicken broth
- 2 carrots (sliced)
- 1 ½ cups white mushrooms (quartered)
- 1 tablespoon vegetable oil
- 2 garlic cloves (chopped)
- 1 cup red wine
- 3 tablespoons cold water
- 1 tablespoon tomato paste
- 1 tablespoon butter
- 2 sprigs thyme
- 1 yellow onion (chopped)
- 1 bay leaf
- 2 tablespoons cornstarch
- 2 tablespoons parsley (chopped)

Instructions

Set the Instant Pot to the browning setting and add the bacon, cooking until crisp and stirring frequently to prevent sticking. Remove the crisped bacon and set to the side, keeping the grease in the pot. Use pepper and salt on the chicken breasts and put this in the pot, browning on each side. Again, leave the fat behind when you remove the chicken to a plate.

Place in the onions and caramelize; six minutes. Add the garlic and cook for an additional minute. Then, put the wine in the pot and use it to deglaze the bottom of the Instant Pot. Allow this to simmer until most of the liquid is evaporated and you have a small amount of concentrated liquid. Then, stir in the tomato paste, chicken broth, carrots, thyme, and bay leaf.

Return the chicken to the cooker and cover, cooking on high pressure for 10 minutes. Use the time you are waiting to warm a skillet over medium-high heat. Add the mushrooms and cook until they start to soften, adding salt and pepper as needed. Use a quick release once the chicken is done and place the chicken in a serving dish.

In a small bowl, whisk together the water and cornstarch. Add this to the cooker and stir well, allowing it to cook on the simmer setting until it thickens. Then, add the mushrooms and coat them with the sauce. Put the prepared mushrooms and sauce over the chicken and top with the chopped parsley and bacon.

♦ *4 servings*

Thai Chicken Thighs

These chicken thighs can be cooked in a fraction of the time it would take to make them in the oven and are topped with a nutty, wholesome sauce. Serve with rice and top with sliced green onions and crunchy peanut pieces.

Ingredients

- ¼ cup peanut butter
- ½ cup chicken broth
- ¼ cup chopped peanuts
- 1 teaspoon ginger
- 2 tablespoons lime juice
- 2 pounds boneless, skinless chicken thighs (trimmed)
- ¼ teaspoon red pepper flakes
- 2 tablespoons canola oil
- 1 tablespoon cilantro
- 2 tablespoons water
- ¼ cup soy sauce
- 1 tablespoon cornstarch

Instructions

Add the oil to the Instant Pot and put on the browning setting. Brown the chicken thighs in batches, laying in a single layer across the pot and removing to a plate when browned. Then, add the cilantro, red pepper, ginger, lime juice, soy sauce, broth, and peanut butter to the pot and mix together. Return the chicken to the pot and set to nine minutes on high.

Use a quick pressure release once the thighs are done and remove the chicken from the pot. In a separate bowl, mix the water and cornstarch until the cornstarch is dissolved. Add this to the pressure cooker and put on the simmer setting. Bring to a boil and allow to thicken. Stir constantly to prevent burning. Once the sauce is thick, return the chicken to the pan and coat. Top with the peanuts.

♦ *4 servings*

Pork Ragu

This is a delicious Italian dish that everybody will love. Simple adjust the red pepper flakes to change the spiciness of your dish.

Ingredients

- 1 tsp oregano
- salt
- 32-oz peeled tomatoes
- 2 carrot, diced
- 1 small onion, diced
- 1 tsp crushed red pepper flakes
- 2 c red wine
- 4 minced cloves garlic
- 2 tbsp olive oil
- 1 tbsp tomato paste
- 2 lb pork loin, cubed

Instructions

Set to sauté. Heat olive oil and brown meat. Add the rest of the ingredients. Lock lid in place. Cook on high, 20 minutes. Release pressure and carefully open. Shred with forks, and serve over pasta.

- *4 servings*

Mongolian Beef

This copycat recipe is very similar to the taste of P.F. Chang's Mongolian beef. Unlike the recipe made in the pan, you add the thickeners after it has been cooked. You lose the crispiness on the outside of the beef, but you gain a lot more tenderness and flavor. You can also prepare this recipe in less than a half hour, which is less than it takes to order most Chinese takeout.

Ingredients

- 2 pounds flank steak
- 4 garlic cloves
- Salt and pepper
- 2 tablespoons cornstarch
- ½ cup + 3 tablespoons water
- ½ cup soy sauce
- 1 tablespoon oil
- 2/3 cup dark brown sugar
- ½ teaspoon fresh ginger (minced)
- 3 green onions (sliced)

Instructions

Start by preparing the beef. Cut the flank steak into ¼ inch thick strips and season with salt and pepper. Add oil to the pressure cooker and set it on the browning setting. Add the steak to the pan once the oil is sizzling and brown with the lid off. Only cook a single layer of the beef at a time (you will probably need to do more than one batch) and transfer to a plate once the meat is browned.

Next, put the garlic in the pan and sauté for a minute. Add the ½ cup water, soy sauce, brown sugar, and ginger to the pot and stir until it is well combined. Clear the settings on the pressure cooker and set it to high pressure. Return the browned beef to the pot and cook for 12 minutes. Once the beep sounds, turn the cooker off and do a quick pressure release. Once the valve has dropped completely, remove the lids.

In a small bowl, add 3 tablespoons of water and the cornstarch. Whisk the mixture until it is smooth and then add to the Instant Pot, stirring constantly. Choose the simmer setting and bring the mixture to a boil, continuing to stir until the sauce becomes thick. When it has cooked for a few minutes, stir in the green onions and serve.

♦ *6 servings*

One Minute Pork Chops with Applesauce

This doesn't take 1-minute start to finish, that's the cook time for the pork chop. You can, however, put a hot meal on the table in less than a half hour with this classic dish that combines sweet apples with versatile pork chops.

Ingredients

- 4 gala apples (cored, peeled, and sliced very thinly)
- 2 tablespoons butter
- 2 tablespoons vegetable oil
- 3 tablespoons water
- 2 garlic cloves (minced)
- ¼ cup soy sauce
- 4 pork loin chops (bone-in, a little more than an inch thick)
- 1 cup chicken stock
- ¼ teaspoon cinnamon
- 1 tablespoon honey
- 1 small onion (thinly sliced)
- 1 tablespoon cornstarch
- Coarse salt and pepper

Instructions

Use the salt and pepper to generously coat your pork chops. Use the sauté setting to brown the chops on each side. Heat oil as hot as you can make it before adding the pork to the pan.

Once the chops are browned, remove them from the pan and set on a plate. Add all of the ingredients except the water and cornstarch to the Instant Pot. Cook for 1 minute and then use a natural release, which should take about 20 minutes. When done, remove the pork chops and set aside.

Whisk the cornstarch and water together in a small bowl until the cornstarch is dissolved. Stir this into the pot and sauté for 2-3 minutes or until your applesauce reaches your desired consistency.

- *4 servings*

Easy Pulled Pork

Traditional pulled pork takes hours to make if you want to achieve juicy, tender, pork that falls apart with the touch of a fork. You can do this in a fraction of the time in your pressure cooker and pair it with your favorite barbecue sauce, either store-bought or one you make on your own.

Ingredients

- ♦ 4 pounds pork shoulder (boneless and halved)
- ♦ 2 tablespoons vegetable oil
- ♦ ½ cup water
- ♦ 2 cups BBQ sauce (divided)

Instructions

Heat the oil on the browning setting in your Instant Pot. Cook the pork one half at a time, browning for about 3 minutes on each side. Remove to a plate once browned. When you are done, add 11/2 cup water and half of the BBQ sauce to the pan, stirring to combine. Add the pork back to the pressure cooker.

Cook for 75 minutes on high pressure. Use a natural release when finished, which will take about 20 minutes. Remove the meat and use two forks to shred, discarding any extra fat you come across. Then, strain the juices out of the pan. Save ½ cup of this.

Mix the shredded pork, the ½ cup cooking liquid, and the remaining barbecue sauce in the pan and stir. Put the pan on the sauté setting until you reach a simmer. Serve on toasted rolls or crusty bread when finished.

♦ *12 servings*

Coconut Lemongrass Chicken

This is a delicious Asian dish that all will love. The lemongrass adds a freshness to this dish, and the coconut adds a sweetness that will make you think you're eating dessert.

Ingredients

- 4 tbsp cilantro
- large onion, sliced
- 1tsp butter
- ½ tsp pepper
- 1 tsp salt
- 10 drumsticks
- 1 c coconut milk
- 1 tsp five spice powder
- 3 tbsp coconut aminos
- small piece ginger, chopped
- 4 crushed garlic cloves
- 2 tbsp fish sauce
- stalk lemongrass, trimmed

Instructions

Smash lemongrass. Combine the ginger, lemongrass, fish sauce, aminos, garlic, and five spice in a food processor. Add milk, mix till smooth. Sprinkle chicken with pepper and salt. Set to sauté and melt the butter. Add onions. Cook till translucent. Add drumsticks and marinade. Lock lid, and set to poultry. When done, turn off and release pressure.

- 5 servings

Lamb with Figs and Ginger

This is a great date night dish for two. It has lots of flavor, and it's healthy. It sounds like it would be a difficult meal to make, but it's a simple one pot meal.

Ingredients

- 5 figs, dried
- ¾ c chicken broth
- 1 tbsp minced ginger
- 2 12-oz lamb shanks
- 1 tsp fish sauce
- 1 medium onion, sliced
- 1 minced garlic clove
- 1 tbsp ACV
- 1 tbsp coconut aminos
- 1 tbsp coconut oil

Instructions

Set to sauté and heat coconut oil. Brown the lamb and put aside. Mix the ginger and onion in the pot. Cook until softened. Mix in garlic, fish sauce, vinegar, and coconut aminos. Stir in figs and broth and deglaze the pot. Place the lamb back in the pot. Seal the lid. Set to high for an hour. Turn off pot and release pressure. Set the shanks aside. Skim off fat from liquid, and serve juice over lamb.

- *2 servings*

Citrus Herb Chicken

The citrus juice adds freshness to the dish. It is perfect for a summer dish, and it's even better when you can use the ingredients when they are in season.

Ingredients

- pepper
- pinch thyme
- 4 tbsp white wine
- 1 tsp chopped rosemary
- 2tsp minced garlic
- ½ c tangerine juice
- salt
- 4 tbsp lemon juice
- 2 lb chicken

Instructions

Put the chicken in the pot. Mix all other ingredients and place on top of the chicken. Lock and seal lid. Select poultry for 15 minutes. Carefully release pressure.

♦ *4 servings*

Pot Roast and Gravy

Who doesn't love a juicy, tender pot roast that has been cooking on low heat in the oven or crock pot all day long? With this pot roast recipe, you do not have to start it in the morning to achieve the wonderful texture that you expect with this tender cut of meat. You can also throw potatoes or vegetables into the pot if you choose.

Ingredients

- 3 ½ pounds rump roast or beef chuck roast
- 1 ½ cup beef broth
- 1 tablespoon cornstarch
- 1 large onion (roughly chopped)
- Lemon pepper seasoning
- 1 tablespoon vegetable oil
- 2 bay leaves
- 3 tablespoon water

Instructions

Pat your meat dry and season it with lemon pepper (unless you have another favorite pot roast seasoning you want to try). Add the oil to the Instant Pot and use the browning function to warm it. Brown the roast on both sides and put on a plate when finished. Add the remaining ingredients to the pot and stir around once or twice to mix. Put your pot roast on top.

Set your pressure cooker for a 70 minute cook time and set on high pressure. Use a natural pressure release for 10 minutes and then use a quick pressure release. Remove to a serving platter, discarding the bay leaves and onion.

Set the Instant Pot to the sauté setting. In a bowl, mix together the cornstarch and water. Add this to the cooking pot when the cornstarch is dissolved and stir. Simmer until the desired consistency of gravy is reached.

- *6 servings*

Sirloin Tips in Gravy

This recipe is delicious served on top of a bed of noodles or mashed potatoes. Add sour cream on top for an extra loving touch. If you have leftovers, you can also use this to make a tasty beef stew.

Ingredients

- 5 pounds sirloin tip roast (cubed)
- 2 cups beef broth
- 1 large onion (diced)
- 3 tablespoons vegetable oil (divided)
- 1 ½ cups water
- ½ cup flour

Instructions

Set the Instant Pot on the browning function and add 1 tablespoon of oil. Once hot, place a single layer of meat across the bottom. You will brown the meat in batches, removing to a separate plate when finished. Once the meat is all cooked, add the onion to the pot and sauté about 5 minutes, until the onion is tender.

Then, return the meat to the pot along with the beef broth and cook for 15 minutes on high pressure. Use a quick pressure release when finished. Whisk the flour and water together quickly, making sure to remove any lumps. Stir this into the cooked meat and set the pot to the browning function. Allow it to come to a boil, stirring continuously until your broth is thick. If needed, add salt and pepper before serving.

- *12 servings*

Stuffed Pepper Casserole

This casserole is reminiscent of a deconstructed stuffed pepper, with the tender but hearty green peppers, flavorful beef, and tender rice. It's also thrown into one convenient pot, so it is faster and a lot less work than traditional stuffed green peppers.

Ingredients

- 1 pound lean ground beef
- ½ cup uncooked rice (long grain)
- Salt and pepper to taste
- 1 cup tomato sauce
- ¼ cup spinach leaves (roughly chopped)
- ½ cup onion (chopped)
- 2 large green peppers (chopped)
- 2 garlic cloves (minced)
- 1 14.5-ounce can tomatoes (leave juices in can)
- 1 cup mozzarella cheese (shredded)
- 1 tablespoon Worcestershire sauce

Instructions

Use the sauté setting to heat the oil in your pot. Add the onion and ground beef, breaking up the beef as it cooks. Once the meat is browned, add the garlic and sauté until fragrant, usually one more minute. Add all of the ingredients except the mozzarella cheese to the pressure cooker and cook for 4 minutes on high pressure.

Use a natural release when the timer goes off. After 10 minutes, use a quick pressure release and turn off the cooker. Grease a baking dish lightly and add the casserole when finished. Top with the mozzarella cheese and put in the broiler until it starts to brown.

- *6 servings*

White Chicken Chili

Chili is a fall favorite but instead of beef in this recipe, you use tender chicken. Normally, this type of chili would take all day to cook but with the pressure cooker, you can have a delicious meal on the table in less than 20 minutes- even less if you cook the chicken beforehand.

Ingredients

- 2 15.5-ounce cans cannellini beans (drained and rinsed)
- 2 cups chicken broth
- 2 garlic cloves (minced)
- 1 4-ounce can green chilies (diced)
- 3 cups chicken (cooked and shredded)
- 1 tablespoon vegetable oil
- 1 teaspoon cumin
- 3 tablespoons cold water
- 1 large onion (diced)
- 2 tablespoons cornstarch
- ¼ teaspoon red pepper flakes
- Salt and pepper to taste

Instructions

Set the Instant Pot to the sauté setting and put the oil inside. Once it is hot, add the onion and cook about 5 minutes, or until tender. Add the garlic and cook until fragrant; about one more minute. Add all of the ingredients except the cornstarch, water, and salt and pepper to the cooker and set on high pressure for five minutes. Turn the cooker off and allow to sit for five minutes, then use a quick pressure release.

While you are waiting, stir the water and cornstarch into a bowl. This will thicken your chili. Stir this in once the lid is off, combining well. Give it a taste test and add salt and pepper as needed.

- *6 servings*

Chicken Cacciatore

This is a quick and delicious Italian dish that children will love. You can easily change the cut of chicken to your favorite.

Ingredients

- ½ c black olives
- 32-oz can stewed tomatoes
- 1 onion, chopped
- 6-12 bone-in drumsticks
- 1 tsp oregano
- bay leaf
- 1 tsp garlic powder
- 1 tsp salt
- 1 c chicken stock

Instructions

Set to sauté. Add in the stock, bay leaf, and salt. Add the following in this order, chicken, onion, garlic, oregano, and then tomatoes. Lock lid, cook on high, 15 minutes. Release pressure, and mix everything together. Meat should fall off bone.

- *8 servings*

Kalua Pork

Traditional Kalua Pork is a Hawaii favorite, involving a 16+ hour process where a pig is wrapped in banana leaves and then smoked for hours in an underground fire pit. This can be made in less than 2 hours with the Instant Pot and it is every bit as tender and flavorful. Serve it over rice with a side of pineapple to enjoy the traditional Hawaiian flavors.

Ingredients

- 4 pounds pork butt roast or pork shoulder roast, halved
- ½ cup water
- 2 tablespoons oil
- 1 tablespoon Hickory flavored liquid smoke
- 2 tablespoons coarse salt

Instructions

Choose the browning setting and add oil to the Instant Pot. Use this to brown the pork when it is hot, browning each half separately. Cook for three minutes on each side and then remove to a plate to cook the other roast. Turn the cooker off and then add liquid smoke and the water to the pot. Mix together and add the browned pieces of roast. Sprinkle the coarse salt on top.

Cook the roast on high pressure for 90 minutes. Use a natural pressure release when it is finished, which will take about 20 minutes. Take the lid off when the valve has dropped completely. Next, take the meat out of the cooker and place in a large bowl. Use two forks to shred the meat, being sure to discard any extra fat chunks that you find. Take some of the juices leftover from cooking and use it to add more moisture to your meat.

- *6 servings*

Sweet and Spicy Orange Chicken

This delicious recipe is sweet with a little kick! You can serve it over rice for a more traditional Asian dish or serve over zucchini and carrot noodles to switch things up. Also, you can top with red pepper flakes or chopped green onions.

Ingredients

- 2 pounds chicken breast (diced)
- ½ cup orange marmalade
- 1 teaspoon sesame oil
- ¼ cup + 3 tablespoons water, divided
- 3 tablespoons cornstarch
- ¼ cup soy sauce
- ¼ teaspoon chili garlic sauce
- 1 tablespoon rice wine vinegar

Instructions

Add all of the ingredients except the cornstarch, 3 tablespoons of water, and marmalade to the pressure cooker. Allow to cook for 3 minutes on high pressure and use the quick pressure release. Put the marmalade in the pot and stir, mixing well.

Let that sit as you dissolve the cornstarch in the water in a small bowl. Mix this into the sauce and put on the sauté setting until it is thick and syrup-like, coating the chicken well.

- *6 servings*

Meatballs

Meatballs are a great dish to have. They can be added to spaghetti or any pasta dish for a great main course. They can also be served by their self as an appetizer.

Ingredients

- onion, diced
- 1 cup water
- ¼ cup breadcrumbs
- 1 ½ cup tomato puree
- 6 tbsp parmesan
- 2 carrots, grated
- oregano
- 1 tsp oil
- pepper
- 1 egg, beaten
- 1 tsp salt, divided
- ¾ lb ground meat
- ¼ c milk

Instructions

Mix together the breadcrumbs, cheese, oregano, half the onion, pepper, and ½ tsp salt. Stir in the meat and milk. Knead the egg into the mixture. Set the pot to sauté and heat the oil. Add in the carrot and the rest of the onion. Stir in the rest of the salt, tomato puree and water.

Form your meatballs now. You can make them any size you want. Place them in the pot as you form them. Seal the lid and set to high for 5 minutes. Let the pressure release naturally. Serve with your choice of pasta or as is.

- *4 servings*

Cherry Apple Pork

Everybody knows that applesauce works well with pork, but this dish proves that cherries work just as well. This dish will satisfy any sweet or savory craving you may be having.

Ingredients

- 1 cup diced apple
- ¼ cup water
- 1/3 cup cherries, pitted
- ¾ lb pork loin
- 3 tbsp onion, diced
- pepper
- 3 tbsp celery, diced
- salt
- ¼ cup apple juice

Instructions

Place all the ingredients into your pot. Seal the lid in place. Set the pot to poultry for 40 minutes. Use the quick pressure release.

- *4 servings*

Apple Pie Pork

This sweet and savory dish combines two things that go great together, pork and apples.

Ingredients

- 4 ¾ lb pork chops
- 2 tbsp AP flour
- ½ tsp allspice
- ½ tsp ground cloves
- ¾ c sugar
- 1 tsp cinnamon
- 6 c sliced apples

Instructions

Cover the apples in all the seasonings and flour. Place the pork chops in the pot. Spread the apple mix over the pork. Seal the lid. Cook for 10 minutes. Carefully release pressure. Serve pork chops covered in apples.

♦ *4 servings*

Chicken Lettuce Wrap

This is a great dish when you in the mood for something light. It's also a great choice for lunch or dinner.

Ingredients

- 4 romaine lettuce leafs
- ½ lb ground chicken
- 2 tbsp chicken broth
- 2 ½ tsp minced garlic
- ¼ c scallions
- 1 tbsp balsamic vinegar
- 1/3 c diced onion
- ¼ tsp ground ginger
- 2 tbsp coconut aminos
- ¼ c drained water chestnuts
- pinch ground allspice

Instructions

Put everything in the pot except for scallions and lettuce. Seal the lid. Cook for 10 minutes, and then quick release. Use a masher to break up the meat. Place meat in the lettuce leaves and top with scallions.

- *2 servings*

Maple Honey Glazed Ham

This a perfect holiday, or special occasion dish, that is quick and easy to make. No need to wait for hours to have your main course.

Ingredients

- bone in ham
- 1 tsp nutmeg
- 2 tbsp orange juice
- ¼ c brown sugar
- 1 tsp cinnamon
- ½ c honey
- ½ c maple syrup

Instructions

Combine everything except for the ham in a pot on medium; mix well. Put the ham in the cooker. Cook 15 minutes, then use quick release. Set the ham in the baking dish. Pour glaze over ham. Place the ham under a broiler to caramelize the sugars and form a slight char.

- *8 servings*

Lemon Mustard Chicken

This chicken will bite you back with its tartness. Mustard adds so much flavor to this dish.

Ingredients

- ♦ salt
- ♦ 2 tbsp lemon juice
- ♦ 1 tbsp olive oil
- ♦ pepper
- ♦ 1 lb chicken thighs
- ♦ 1 tbsp Italian seasoning
- ♦ 1 tbsp Dijon
- ♦ 1/3 c chicken broth
- ♦ 1 lb red potatoes, quartered

Instructions

Mix together the broth, juice, and mustard. Place oil in pot. Season chicken with pepper and salt. Place in pot. Pour broth mix over chicken. Add potatoes and Italian seasoning. Cover, cook on high, 15 minutes.

♦ *2 servings*

Beef Stroganoff

This is the best comfort food. It's perfect for a cold winter night to warm up by. This isn't your grandmother's stroganoff.

Ingredients

- 12-oz egg noodles, cooked
- ½ tsp pepper
- 8-oz sour cream
- 4 tbsp red wine
- 2 minced garlic clove
- 1 large onion, sliced
- ½ tsp thyme
- ¼ tsp paprika
- 1 1/3 c beef stock
- ½ tsp rosemary
- 1 tsp salt
- ¾ c flour
- olive oil
- ½ tsp onion powder
- 2 lb sirloin tip roast

Instructions

Shake the dry ingredients in bag. Add the beef and coat. Set to sauté and heat 2 tbsp oil. In batches, brown meat. Set to the side. Place the onions in the pot, cook until translucent. Mix in garlic. Mix in beef, wine, and stock. Seal lid, cook on high, 20 minutes. Release pressure. Mix a little liquid at a time into sour cream until it has warmed. Mix into the meat mixture. Stir in pepper and salt. Serve over noodles.

◆ *4 servings*

French Dip Sandwiches

This is a great option for lunch, and it keeps well if there are any leftovers. This is a perfect addition at a picnic or a party.

Ingredients

- hamburger buns
- 1 tsp minced garlic
- 2 tsp peppercorns
- 1 tsp beef bouillon
- ¾ c soy sauce
- 1 tbsp rosemary
- 4 lb roast beef

Instructions

Trim fat off roast and place in pot. Stir together garlic, rosemary, peppercorns, bouillon, and soy sauce. Pour on the roast. Pour in water to cover the roast. Seal lid in place. Set to beef for 35 minutes. Carefully release pressure. Shred the beef and serve on hamburger buns.

- *8 servings*

Brown sugar Garlic Chicken

This is the perfect mixture of sweet and savory. The soda in this dish adds an extra layer of flavor that nobody will be able to guess.

Ingredients

- 1 tsp pepper
- 2 tbsp soy sauce
- 4tbsp lemon lime soda
- 6 tbsp vinegar
- 2 tsp minced garlic
- 6 tbsp brown sugar
- 1 lb chicken

Instructions

Place everything in the pot and seal the lid. Select poultry for 15 minutes. Quick release the pressure

- *4 servings*

Jambalaya

This is a delicious Creole dish that brings New Orleans to your home. Everybody will love the flavor and meatiness this dish contains.

Ingredients

- ½ lb andouille sausage
- 1 ½ tsp Worcestershire sauce
- 1 c onion, diced
- 2 ¼ tbsp Creole seasoning
- ½ c crushed tomatoes
- 1 ½ c chicken stock
- ½ lb chicken, diced
- ¾ c rice
- 1 tbsp garlic, minced
- 1 c bell peppers
- ½ lb prawns
- olive oil

Instructions

Set to sauté. Sprinkle the chicken with 1 tsp Creole seasoning, brown. Remove chicken. Place garlic, onions, and pepper, let cook until soft. Mix in rice, cook for two more minutes. Mix in chicken, Worcestershire, remaining Creole, and tomato puree. Cover, and set to rice. Release steam, add prawns and sausage. Cover, press manual, cook 2 minutes.

♦ *6 servings*

Ranch Pork Chops

This is a quick, last minute dish, with minimal ingredients. Flavors can be mixed up by changing the ranch dressing mix for any dry flavor mix of your choice.

Ingredients

- 1 2/3 c water
- 10oz cream of chicken
- 1 oz ranch dressing mix
- 2 lb boneless pork chops

Instructions

Mix everything in pot and seal lid. Set to meat for 15 minutes. Quick release the pressure.

- *4 servings*

Maple Brisket

This brisket is a tough meal to prepare, but with this recipe is quick, easy, and fool-proof. This also makes for great leftover sandwiches.

Ingredients

- 4 thyme sprigs
- 1 tsp mustard powder
- 1 tbsp liquid smoke
- 1 tsp onion powder
- 1 tsp pepper
- ½ tsp paprika
- 2 tsp salt
- 2 c broth
- 2 tbsp maple sugar
- 2 lb beef brisket

Instructions

Mix dry spices together and rub into brisket. Set pot to sauté. Grease pot with oil and brown brisket. Lay brisket fat side up, and throw in the thyme, broth, and liquid smoke. Set to high for 40 minutes. Once finished, let pressure release naturally. Remove and cover with foil.

Optional: Turn to sauté and reduce left over liquid.

Slice brisket and drizzle with liquid.

- *8 servings*

Creamy Pork Chops

There is no shortage of flavor in this dish. The soup and sour cream adds a creaminess to the pork chops and allows the natural flavors to shine through.

Ingredients

- 2 tsp parsley
- 1 ½ c sour cream
- 8 pork chops
- cream of mushroom soup
- 1 ½ c water
- 2tsp chicken bouillon
- 2 tbsp oil
- pepper

Instructions

Set pot to sauté. Heat the oil. Season chops with pepper and brown in pot. Set aside. Add bouillon and water and deglaze. Place the chops back in. Lock lid, cook on high, 8 minutes. Turn off. Release pressure. Remove chops and keep warm. Mix in soup and sour cream. Stir parsley and serve over chops.

- *4-8 servings*

Buffalo Chicken

A spicy, delicious, and easy to make dish perfect for a party or a weeknight dinner. You can easily change the buffalo sauce to any type of sauce you desire to create an entirely different meal

Ingredients

- 1 oz ranch dressing mix
- 12 fl oz buffalo sauce
- 3 lbs chicken breasts

Instructions

Put all of the ingredients in you pot. Seal the lid. Set to poultry for 15 minutes. Carefully release pressure. Shred the chicken and serve covered in sauce.

- *4 servings*

Santa Fe Chicken

This is a delicious tex-mex chicken dish. The spice level can easily be adjusted for your taste by adjusting the amount of cayenne you add. You can also use diced tomatoes without the chiles to reduce the heat.

Ingredients

- 1 lb chicken
- 4 c corn chips
- 10 oz diced tomatoes with green chiles
- salt
- 1 tsp onion powder
- 10 fl oz chicken broth
- 1 tsp cayenne
- 1 tsp cumin
- 6 tbsp diced scallion
- 1 tsp garlic powder
- 1 c corn
- 14 oz black beans
- 1 tsp dried cilantro

Instructions

Mix the seasonings, onions, corn, beans, tomatoes, and broth in the pot. Set chicken on top. Seal the lid in place. Set to poultry for 10 minutes. Quick release the pressure. Take out the chicken and shred. Mix back into the pot, and serve with corn chips.

- *4 servings*

Root Beer Pork

This is a great backyard barbecue dish. This makes for a great main attraction at a summer pool party. The root beer adds an extra flavor to the pork that nobody will expect.

Ingredients

- 2 lb pork roast
- 1 tbsp honey
- ½ tsp garlic salt
- 2 tbsp tomato paste
- ½ tsp pepper
- 1 1/3 cup onion, sliced
- ½ tsp lemon juice
- ¾ cup root beer
- 1 tbsp Worcestershire sauce
- 1 tbsp flour
- 4 tbsp ketchup

Instructions

Sprinkle pork with pepper and garlic slat. Place the pork in the pot. Combine all the rest of the ingredient and place over top of the pork. Seal the lid in place. Set your pot to meat/stew for 35 minutes. Release the pressure.

Remove the onion and the pork. Shred the pork and mix back into the mixture.

♦ *6 servings*

Tomato and Porcini Short Ribs

This is a great Italian take on short ribs. The marinara and balsamic gives sweetness to the dish, while the mushrooms adds an extra meatiness.

Ingredients

- 4 tbsp Italian parsley
- 4 lbs short ribs, 4 inch segments
- ½ c chicken broth
- 1 large onion, chopped
- salt
- 1 c marinara sauce
- pepper
- 6 cloves garlic, smashed
- ½ oz porcini mushrooms
- 2 celery stalk, chopped
- 2 tbsp balsamic vinegar, divided
- 2 carrot, chopped
- 1 tbsp butter
- 1 c boiling water

Instructions

Season ribs with pepper and salt. Put the mushrooms in a bowl with boiling water and let them set 15 minutes. Set pot to sauté and heat butter. Sear ribs on all sides. Set aside. Put the veggies in the pot and sprinkle with pepper and salt. Cook until soft. Drain mushrooms and chop. Add them and the garlic to the veggies. Add the broth, marinara, and half the balsamic. Add the ribs into mixture. Bring mixture to boil. Seal lid in place. Set to high and cook 35 minutes. Release pressure. Add the rest of the balsamic, and season if needed.

- *6 servings*

Johnny Marzetti

This a dish that, unfortunately, not many people know about. It's a perfect dish when you're unsure of what you want to eat. It's also great to use up extra leftovers you may have.

Ingredients

- 8 oz cheddar cheese
- 3 c ground beef, cooked
- 16 oz egg noodles, cooked
- 1 c onion, diced
- 2 tbsp cornstarch
- 32 oz diced tomatoes
- 2 tsp sugar
- 3 c sliced bell pepper
- 4 tbsp soy sauce
- 4 tbsp water
- 2 beef bouillon cube
- ½ tsp garlic powder

Instructions

Mix together the water, bouillon, garlic powder, tomatoes, onions, and ground beef in the pot. Seal the lid in place and set for 10 minutes. Quick release the pressure. Stir in the green peppers, cornstarch, sugar, and soy sauce. Set to sauté for 5 minutes. Cook noodles as directed by package. Stir in the cheese with the noodles. Serve beef mixture on the noodles.

- *6 servings*

Steak

Everybody thinks a steak has to be cooked on a grill to be good. This recipe is here to prove them wrong. You can have a delicious, flavorful steak with your Instant Pot.

Ingredients

- 2 tbsp onion soup mix
- 2 lb flank steak
- ½ cup oil
- 1 tbsp Worcestershire sauce
- 4tbsp ACV

Instructions

Set you pot to sauté. Once hot, brown your steak on each side. Mix in the Worcestershire, oil, onion soup mix, and vinegar. Seal the lid and set to meat/stew for 35 minutes. Release the pressure.

- *4 servings*

Bacon Spaghetti

This is a delicious take on spaghetti. This will give you a break from the regular red sauce dish, that everybody knows, by adding in everybody's favorite meat, bacon.

Ingredients

- 8 oz spaghetti
- ¾ c diced bacon
- 2 tsp salt
- pinch garlic powder
- 1 ¼ c diced onion
- ¼ tsp ground cloves
- ½ tsp cinnamon
- ¼ tsp pepper
- 1 ½ c ground beef, cooked
- 2 tsp celery seed
- 6 oz tomato paste
- ½ tsp paprika
- 2 tsp sugar
- 32 fl oz tomato juice
- 2 tbsp parsley
- 1 ½ tsp Worcestershire sauce

Instructions

Set the pot to sauté and cook the bacon. Remove bacon leaving behind the drippings. Cook onions in drippings, 2 minutes. Add back the bacon and the rest of the ingredients, minus the noodles. Seal the lid in place. Set pot to meat and cook 15 minutes. Prepare noodles according to package. Quick release the sauce and pour over noodles.

- *2 servings*

Honey Bourbon Chicken

This sweet chicken is a delicious main course. Contrary to the title, there is absolutely no bourbon in this dish.

Ingredients

- 2 lb chicken
- 1 tbsp water
- 2 tsp garlic, minced
- salt
- 2 tbsp cornstarch
- pepper
- ¼ tsp red pepper flake
- ½ cup onion, diced
- 1 cup honey
- 2 tbsp oil
- ½ cup soy sauce
- 4 tbsp ketchup

Instructions

Put everything in your cooker except for the cornstarch and water. Seal the lid and set to chicken for 15 minutes. If your chicken is frozen, add an extra 10 minutes. Release the pressure. Take out the chicken and shred.

Set to sauté. Combine the cornstarch and water. Mix the slurry and the chicken back into the liquid. Let it cook for a few minutes to thicken.

- *4 servings*

Korean Beef

This easy and quick take on this tasty Korean dish makes it an obvious choice for dinner any time of the week.

Ingredients

- 1 small orange, juiced
- 3 tbsp soy sauce
- 1 ½ tsp olive oil
- 1 small apple, chopped and peeled
- ¼ c beef broth
- ½ tsp grated ginger
- pepper
- 2 garlic cloves, minced
- salt
- 1 lb bottom roast, cubed

Instructions

Season roast with pepper and salt. Heat pot to sauté, coat with oil, and brown meat in batches. Deglaze pot with broth, scrap up browned bits. Mix in soy sauce. Place the meat back in the pot and add ginger, apple, and garlic; mix. Lastly, mix in orange juice. Cover and seal lid. Set to normal pressure for 45 minutes. When finished, release pressure and shred meat. Serve with rice.

- *2 servings*

BBQ Beef Sandwiches

This a great dish for any time of the year. This is simple with minimal ingredients, and even the kids will love it.

Ingredients

- 2 lb beef roast
- buns
- 1 cup barbecue sauce

Instructions

Trim any excess fat from the meat. Put the meat and your choice of sauce in the pot. Seal the lid in place and set for 40 minutes. Release the pressure. Shred the meat and place on the hamburger buns.

- *6 servings*

Garlic Lemon Chicken

This healthy chicken recipes is full of flavor. Chicken in the Instant Pot cooks much faster than baked chicken does, so you'll be able to devour the delicious meal faster.

Ingredients

- 2 lbs chicken breasts
- 4 tbsp arrowroot flour
- 1 tsp sea salt
- lemon, juiced
- medium onion, diced
- ¼ cup white wine
- 1 tbsp butter
- ½ tsp paprika
- 6 garlic cloves minced
- 1 tsp parsley
- ½ cup chicken broth

Instructions

Set your pot to sauté and melt the butter. Cook the onions until they have softened. Mix in everything else except for the flour. Seal the lid and set to poultry. Use quick pressure release. Remove ¼ cup of the sauce and mix it with the flour. Pour in the pot and stir everything together. Allow to thicken for a minute.

- *6 servings*

Pork Carnitas

These are perfect served on their own or in a tortilla with extra toppings. However you seem them, they are sure to be a hit.

Ingredients

- ½ tsp garlic powder
- 1 bay leaf
- pepper
- 2 chipotle pepper
- ½ c chicken broth
- salt
- ¼ tsp oregano
- ½ tsp sazon
- ¼ tsp dry adobo
- ½ tsp cumin
- 2 sliced garlic clove
- 1 pound pork shoulder

Instructions

Sprinkle salt and pepper over pork. Set instant pot to sauté and brown pork. Remove from pot and cool. Cut pockets in pork to insert slices of garlic. Season with garlic powder, cumin, adobo, oregano, and sazon. Put broth, chipotle, and bay leaf in pot and mix. Place pork in pot, cover and seal. Set to high pressure for 50 minutes. Once done and pressure has released, shred with fork. Remove bay leaf, and mix meat back in juices. Adjust seasonings as needed.

- *4 servings*

Salsa Verde Chicken

This delicious tex-mex dish will be a hit with your whole family. It's delicious, healthy, and quick to fix.

Ingredients

- 8 oz salsa verde
- ½ tsp salt
- ½ tsp paprika
- ½ tsp cumin
- 1 lb boneless chicken breast

Instructions

Put everything in cooker. Set to high for 25 minutes. Once finished, quick release pressure and shred chicken.

- *4 servings*

Cassoulet

This delicious French dish isn't hard to make at all. It's quick and easy to make and is full of delicious flavor

Ingredients

- 2 c herb croutons
- 1 celery stalk, diced
- 4 minced garlic cloves
- 2 tbsp rosemary
- ½ onion, diced
- 2 carrot, diced
- 2 c great northern beans
- 2 lb pork ribs, chunked
- 1 c beef broth
- 2tbsp olive oil

Instructions

Heat cooker to sauté. Season ribs with pepper and salt and brown in pot. Add broth, celery, beans, carrot, rosemary, garlic, and onion. Seal pot and cook 35 minutes. Serve with croutons.

- *4 servings*

Shrimp Boil

A fast and easy way to have a shrimp boil right at home. No need for elaborate outdoor boil pots or anything.

Ingredients

- 4 c water
- 1 ½ lb shrimp, unpeeled
- 1 ½ tbsp old bay
- 1 ½ oz crab boil seasoning bag
- 8 mini corn cobs
- 2 ½ lb small potatoes
- 1 lb smoked sausage

Ingredients

Cut the sausage into chunks and put in a bag. Keep the boil bag together. Place the crab boil, old bay, corn cobs, and potatoes into the sausage bag and coat. Put everything in the bag in your cooker and pour in the water. Set to slow cook for 6-8 hours on low. Mix in the shrimp and cook 30 minutes.

♦ *8 servings*

Shrimp Creole

This spicy shrimp dish is delicious and full of flavor. The spiciness can be adjust with an adjustment of the cayenne.

Ingredients

- 2 c cooked rice
- 2 tbsp parsley
- ¼ tsp salt
- 1 oz diced tomatoes
- 2 tbsp butter
- 2 garlic cloves, minced
- ½ c sweet pepper
- ½ c celery, chopped
- 1/8 tsp cayenne
- ½ tsp paprika
- onion, chopped
- 1 lb shrimp, cleaned

Instructions

Mix everything except for the shrimp in the pot. Set to slow cook. Let cook 40 minutes on low. Place the shrimp and cook additional 20 minutes.

- *6 servings*

Shrimp Scampi

This delicious Italian dish is full of flavor. The butter adds a richness while the lemon and garlic adds flavor and spice.

Ingredients

- 1 lb raw shrimp, cleaned
- 2 tbsp oil
- 2 tbsp parsley
- 1 tbsp garlic, minced
- salt
- 1 tbsp lemon juice
- ½ c white cooking wine
- pepper
- ¼ c chicken broth
- 2 tbsp butter

Instructions

Mix together the pepper, salt, lemon juice, parsley, garlic, butter, oil, wine, and broth in your cooker. Mix in the shrimp. Set to slow cook for 2 ½ hours on low.

- *6 servings*

Spicy Citrus Fish

This easily adjustable seafood dish is delicious and easy to make. It makes perfect use of the slow cook setting.

Ingredients

♦ your choice of fish
♦ pineapple salsa
♦ orange juice
♦ coconut milk
♦ fresh vegetables of your choosing

Instructions

Put the vegetables in the bottom of your cooker. Pour over the juices and part of the salsa. Set to slow cook for 2 ½ hours on low. Put the rest of the salsa in the pot with the fish. Set to high and cook 40 minutes.

♦ *4 servings*

Steamed Mussels

As fast and simple way to make delicious steamed mussls. It adds plenty of flavor with the wine and chile.

Ingredients

- ¼ c parsley, chopped
- ½ c dry white wine
- 2 lb mussels
- ¼ tsp pepper
- ¼ tsp salt
- Serrano chile, chopped
- ¼ c shallots, minced
- 1 tbsp butter

Instructions

Put everything the cooker. Set to slow cook and set for an hour on low. Check periodical and stop cooking once the mussels have opened.

- *Servings vary*

Lasagna Pie

This is a quick and easy lasagna that everybody will love. You can change up the ingredients to suit your taste

Ingredients

- Fresh mushrooms
- Italian sausage, ground
- Shredded parmesan
- Ricotta
- Jar pasta sauce
- Dry lasagna noodles

Instructions

Spray springform with cooking spray. Add a layer of noodles on the bottom. Add a little ricotta and sauce. Add some sausage, shredded cheese, and mushrooms. Another layer of noodles, repeat as before; continue until you've used all ingredients. Top with foil. Set trivet and 1 ½ c water in pot. Place lasagna on trivet. Cook on high, 20 minutes. Natural pressure release. Set for 10 minutes.

♦ *4 servings*

Thai Lime Chicken

This zesty chicken is sure to be a crowd pleaser. The freshness of the mint, the zip of the ginger, and sweetness of the coconut combines great together.

Ingredients

- 1 tsp cilantro
- ½ tsp mint
- ½ tsp ginger
- 1 tbsp coconut nectar
- 2 tbsp olive oil
- ¼ c fish sauce
- ½ c lime juice
- 1 lb boneless chicken thighs

Instructions

Put the chicken in the pot. Combine the rest of the ingredients. Place on top of the chicken. Choose poultry and cook 10 minutes. Quick release pressure.

- *2 servings*

Salt Baked Chicken

This is an interesting and tasteful chicken dish. The layer of seasonings add lots of flavor to the chicken.

Ingredients

- pepper
- ¼ tsp five spice powder
- 1 tsp salt
- 2 tsp dried sand ginger
- 8 chicken legs

Instructions

Coat chicken with ginger, salt, five spice powder; mix. Wrap chicken in parchment paper. Place in a shallow dish. Put steamer rack in pot with a cup water. Add the dish of chicken on rack. Cook on high, 20 minutes. Slowly release pressure.

- *4 servings*

Filipino Chicken Adobo

This chicken is full of flavor and spice. This is a delicious recipe when served with rice.

Ingredients

- 1 bay leaf
- ¼ c white vinegar
- ½ tsp pepper
- 2 crushed garlic cloves
- ¼ c soy sauce
- 2 lbs chicken thighs

Instructions

Set pot to poultry. Place everything in the pot. Seal lid, set to high, 15 minutes.

- *2 servings*

Bolognese

The delicious Bolognese sauce is perfect served over spaghetti or any of your favorite pasta.

Ingredients

- 2 tsp sugar
- 1 c crushed tomatoes
- 1 tbsp minced garlic
- 4 tbsp red wine
- ½ tsp Italian seasoning
- ½ tsp pepper
- ½ lb ground chunk
- ½ lb spicy pork sausage
- 1 tsp salt
- 1 c chopped onion
- 1 tsp ground fennel
- ½ c celery
- ½ c carrots
- 2 tbsp olive oil

Instructions

Set to sauté, add oil. Add celery, onions, garlic, and carrots until soft. Add meat and seasonings. Brown meat. Deglaze with red wine, cook 15 minutes. Mix in sugar and tomatoes. Lock lid, cook on high, 15 minutes.

Indian Curry

This spicy dish is great when you're in the mood for something different. Adjust the amount of curry and chili powder to adjust the heat.

Ingredients

- salt
- 1 ¼ c water
- pepper
- 1/3 c tomato paste
- 1 tbsp ginger
- 1 medium shallot
- 1 tbsp cilantro
- ¼ tsp Indian chili powder
- 3 tbsp curry powder
- 2 tbsp olive oil
- 1 medium potato
- 2 small onions
- 8 garlic cloves
- 2 c goat shoulder

Instructions

Set to sauté. Add olive oil and goat. Sprinkle with pepper and salt. Brown shoulder. Set aside. Add olive oil, ginger, shallot, and onion and stir. Mix in garlic, cook until fragrant. Stir in curry, and chili pepper until fragrant. Add ¼ c water and deglaze pot. Mix in the rest of the water. Add goat and tomato paste. Don't stir. Add potatoes. Cover and lock lid. Cook on high, 36 minutes. Turn off and let pressure release. Break up potato to thicken sauce. Stir in cilantro.

♦ *2 servings*

Barbacoa de Cordero

Everybody loves goo barbacoa and this one has all the right seasonings. It's simple and easy to make, and you're sure to make it again and again.

Ingredients

- salt
- 2tbsp oil
- 16-oz can enchilada sauce
- 2 minced garlic cloves
- 2 small onion
- 2lb lamb shoulder

Instructions

Marinate the lamb in enchilada sauce. Set to sauté. Add oil. Cook onion until soft, then add garlic. Add lamb and sauce. Bring to boil. Set to stew, cook 36 minutes. Shred cooked lamb. Serve as you desire.

- *4 servings*

Sous Vide Duck

This difficult French dish just became easier. It's delicious, and moist, and full of flavor.

Ingredients

- 1 tbsp vegetable oil
- 1/3 tsp thyme
- ½ tsp pepper
- 1/3 tsp peppercorn
- 2 tsp minced garlic
- 1 tsp salt
- 2 boneless duck breasts

Instructions

Rub duck with spices. Chill for two hours. Rinse off spices. Put duck in bag, remove air when sealing. Add water in pot to 7 cup mark. Turn to keep warm. Leave for 20 minutes. Put bag in water for 38 minutes. Take the bag out, and pat the breasts dry. Sear the skin of the duck in a pan with oil. Flip and cook 20 more seconds.

♦   *2 servings*

Duck a l'Orange

This, typically, tricky dish just became a lot easier. You set it and forget, and before you know it, you have a delicious meal that your friend won't believe you made.

Ingredients:

♦ 1 can orange juice concentrate
♦ 1 onion, cut in eights
♦ 1 apple, sliced
♦ 2 oranges, peeled and sliced
♦ ¼ tsp pepper
♦ ½ tsp salt
♦ 2 duck breasts, cut in half

Instructions

Season the duck with pepper and salt. Place in the duck, then oranges, then the apples, and lastly the onion. Pour the orange juice over everything. Set to slow cook for 8-10 hours on low. Take out the duck and discard the leftover liquid.

♦ *2 servings*

Spicy Chicken

This chicken is full of flavor and full of spice. This delicious dish can be served over rice if desired.

Ingredients

- pinch salt
- 2 garlic cloves, minced
- pinch pepper
- 1 tsp cumin
- onion, chopped
- 1 tsp chili powder
- ¼ c tomato sauce
- ½ jar salsa
- 3 boneless chicken breasts

Instructions

Put your chicken in your pot. Top with tomato sauce and salsa. Mix in the cumin, salt, chili powder, pepper, onion, and garlic. Set to slow cook for 4-5 hours on low. Remove chicken and shred then mix back into mixture.

Thanksgiving Turkey

This recipe makes for a quick and easy Thanksgiving. No need to baby sit the turkey. It's sure to be juice.

Ingredients

- 1 tsp dried sage
- 2 tbsp AP flour
- 1 can turkey gravy
- 1 tbsp Worcestershire sauce
- ½ tsp garlic pepper
- 1 bone in turkey breast
- 5 slices bacon

Instructions

Crisp the bacon in a pan and crumble. Coat your cooker with nonstick spray. Put the turkey in the pot. Sprinkle over with garlic. Combine the sage, Worcestershire, flour, gravy, and bacon together. Place this mixture on the turkey. Set to slow cook on low for 8 hours.

- *12 servings*

Leg of Lamb

This is a delicious and easy way to fix lamb. Everybody will love it, and it keeps well for leftovers.

Ingredients

♦ onion, sliced
♦ 5 c water
♦ 2 garlic cloves, minced
♦ ½ c soy sauce
♦ 1 pkg onion soup mix
♦ 4 lbs leg of lamb, rolled

Instructions

Put everything in the pot and combine. Set to slow cook for 8-10 hours on low. Take out lamb and allow it to rest a few minutes before slicing.

♦ *4 servings*

Red Curry Pulled Pork

This spicy pork dish is a delicious dinner, or lunch. Spice levels can easily be adjust to fit your taste.

Ingredients

- salt
- 4 tsp oil
- 2 tbsp + 2 tsp lime juice
- ¼ c cilantro, chopped
- 1 c carrot, shredded
- 2 c cabbage, sliced
- lime zest
- ¼ c coconut milk
- 2 baguettes
- 3 ½ lb boneless pork shoulder
- 1 ½ tbsp fish sauce
- ¼ c thai red curry paste, divided
- ¼ c lime juice
- ¼ c brown sugar, packed

Instructions

Mix together fish sauce, brown sugar, 3 tbsp curry paste, and ¼ c lime juice in the cooker. Place in the pork and coat in mixture. Set to slow cook and set to high for four hours. Take out the pork. For the slaw, mix together the salt, oil, lime juice, cilantro, carrot, and cabbage. Cut baguettes in 5 pieces. Toast them if you want. Take the pork and shred it. Mix it back into the sauce along with 1 tbsp curry paste, lime zest, and coconut milk. Mix well. Place on the baguette along with the slaw.

♦ *4 servings*

Rosemary Lamb

The delicious dish is perfect for the holidays. The rosemary will make it look just like a wreath.

Ingredients

- 2 tbsp butter, melted
- 1 tsp pepper
- ½ tbsp garlic, minced
- 3 tsp Worcestershire sauce
- 1 lb baby carrots
- ¼ tsp oregano
- 1 lb onions, quartered
- 1 tbsp rosemary
- 1.5 lb potatoes, quartered
- 1 tsp paprika
- 1.5 lb lamb, cubed
- 4 c beef broth

Instructions

Place the following ingredients in cooker as such: broth, potato, onion, carrot, lamb. Drizzle with Worcestershire, and sprinkle over with the spices. Pour the melted butter over everything. Set to slow cook for 8 hours on low.

- *5 servings*

Barley Chickpea Risotto

This is a delicious vegetarian main dish that even meat eaters will enjoy devouring.

Ingredients

- 3 tbsp parsley, chopped
- 1/3 c parmesan
- ½ tsp salt
- 1 ¼ c water
- 2 ½ c vegetable broth
- 3 carrots, chopped
- 1 can garbanzo beans, rinsed
- 1 ½ tbsp lemon juice
- ½ head cauliflower, chopped
- 1 ¼ c pearl barley
- 4 thyme sprigs
- ½ onion, minced
- ¼ tsp pepper
- 3 garlic cloves, minced
- 1 ½ tbsp EVOO

Ingredients

Heat skillet with oil and place in onion, cauliflower, garlic, and carrots. Let the vegetables cook until soft. Mix in the barley and thyme. Place the veggie mixture in your cooker. Mix in the pepper, salt, water, broth, and beans. Set to slow cook for 2-2 ½ hours on high. All liquid should be absorbed. Takeout the thyme sprigs. Mix in the lemon juice.

- *4 servings*

Eggplant Parmesan

Healthy version of chicken parmesan. People that eat it won't even realize it's vegetarian.

Ingredients

♦ package mozzarella, sliced
♦ 32 oz jar marinara sauce
♦ 1/3 c water
♦ ½ c parmesan, grated
♦ 1/3 c breadcrumbs, seasoned
♦ 3 tbsp AP flour
♦ 2 eggs
♦ 1 tbsp salt
♦ 4 eggplant, peeled and sliced
♦ 1 c EVOO

Instructions

Layer the eggplant slices in a bowl. Season every layer with salt. Let the eggplant sit for 30 minutes. Drain and rinse the eggplant. Heat oil in a pan. Mix together the flour, water, and eggs. Coat the eggplant in egg and brown each sides in the skillet. Mix the parmesan and breadcrumbs together. Put a layer of eggplant in your cooker. Sprinkle with breadcrumbs. Pour on some marinara and sprinkle with mozzarella. Continue layering this way until all ingredients are used. Set to slow cook for 4-5 hour on low.

♦ *6 servings*

Picadillo Stuffed Peppers

This is a one pot dish. The filling in the peppers are vegan friendly, and is loaded with flavor

Ingredients

- ¼ c raisins
- 1/3 c onion, chopped
- 2 c rice, cooked
- ½ bell peppers
- 4 lg bell peppers
- ¼ tsp cinnamon
- 1 tsp cumin
- 1 tbsp red wine vinegar
- 26 oz jar marinara sauce

Instructions

Mix together the cinnamon, cumin, vinegar, and marinara sauce. Place 1 1/3 cups of this mixture in the pot. Chop up the bell pepper half. Trim top off the pepper and clean out seeds. Mix together the remaining sauce, chopped pepper, raisins, onion, and rice. Place this mixture inside of the pepper and place their tops back on them. Put the peppers in the pot. Place on slow cook on low for six to eight hours. Serve with the sauce and parsley.

♦ *4 servings*

Quinoa Black Bean Peppers

Another vegan stuffed pepper recipe that everybody will enjoy eating. Most won't even realize there isn't any meat

Ingredients

- 1 ½ c pepperjack, shredded
- 1 c quinoa, rinsed
- ½ tsp garlic salt
- 1 tsp onion powder
- 14 oz can refried beans
- 1 tsp cumin
- 1 tsp chili powder
- 14 oz can black beans, rinsed
- 6 bell peppers
- 1 ½ c red enchilada sauce

Instructions

Remove the tops for the peppers and take out the seeds and ribs. Mix together 1 cup of cheese, spices, enchilada sauce, beans, and quinoa. Spoon the mixture into each pepper. Place a half a cup of water in the cooker. Set the peppers in the water. Set to slow cook. Set for six hours; low, or three hours; high. Top with remaining cheese. Top with desired toppings such as sour cream, avocado, or cilantro.

- *6 servings*

Vegan Jambalaya

Jambalaya is a delicious meal, but not everybody wants all the meats that are in it, so this recipe solves that problem

Ingredients

- ♦ 1 c rice
- ♦ ½ tsp oregano
- ♦ 1 ½ tsp Cajun seasoning
- ♦ 1 tbsp miso paste
- ♦ 3 celery stalks, chopped
- ♦ ½ lg green bell pepper, chopped
- ♦ ½ onion, chopped
- ♦ 8 oz smoked vegan sausage, sliced
- ♦ 2 garlic cloves, minced
- ♦ 1 c vegetable broth
- ♦ 8 oz seitan, cubed
- ♦ 28 oz diced tomatoes
- ♦ 1 tbsp oil

Instructions

Drizzle the oil on the bottom of your cooker. Mix together everything, except the rice, in the pot. Set to slow cook on low, four hours. Mix in the rice. Turn temp to high, cook 30 minutes.

♦ *6 servings*

Baked Spaghetti

Baked spaghetti that never has to go into the oven, it is all done in your Instant Pot with all flavor of baked

Ingredients

- ½ c parmesan
- 1 tbsp oil
- 4 oz fontina cheese
- 8 oz mozzarella
- 24 oz jar fire roasted tomato sauce
- 2 tsp garlic, minced
- 8 oz prechopped onion/bell pepper mix
- 1 lb Italian sausage
- 8 oz spaghetti

Instructions

Spray pot with cooking spray. Place the noodles on the bottom of the pot and spread remaining ingredients on top, except the cheeses. Mix the cheeses together and springs on top. Set to slow cook for 3 hours on low. Allow to stand for 10 minutes.

♦ *6 servings*

Provincial Chicken

Typically a fancy dish that is difficult to make, but this recipe makes it easy to do with minimal prep.

Ingredients

- bowtie pasta
- ½ c sour cream
- 1 tsp basil
- 2 tbsp parsley
- 1 tbsp dried onion, minced
- 2 tbsp balsamic vinegar
- 1 c cheddar cheese
- can cream of chicken soup
- 2 zucchini, diced
- 2 cans diced tomatoes
- 4 boneless chicken breasts

Instructions

Mix together the herbs, onion, vinegar, soup, zucchini, tomatoes, chicken, and pasta in the cooker. Set to slow cook on low, six to eight hours. Take out the chicken and dice. Place back in the cooker with the sour cream and cheese. Mix everything together and cook for another 15 minutes.

- *4 servings*

Quinoa and Sausage

A spicy dish that is healthy and is full of flavor. Everybody will enjoy eating it.

Ingredients

- 1 c cheddar cheese
- 2 packages Italian chicken sausage links
- onion, cut into wedges
- 3 sweet peppers, diced
- 2 tsp honey
- 2 tbsp stone ground mustard
- ¼ c cider vinegar
- 1 c quinoa
- can chicken broth

Instructions

In your cooker mix together the honey, mustard, vinegar, quinoa, and broth. Stir in the sausage, sweet peppers, and onions. Set to slow cook. Let cook four to five hours on low. Top with cheese.

♦ *4 servings*

Quinoa Casserole

A healthy, vegan friendly, dish that doesn't take too much time to throw together.

Ingredients

- 2 tbsp oregano, chopped
- 1 bell pepper, chopped
- 2 lb summer squash, diced
- 1 tbsp lime juice
- 1 c crumbled feta cheese
- 1 c quinoa
- 1 tsp salt
- ½ c onion, chopped
- 1 pint cherry tomatoes
- 12 oz tomatillos, husked and chopped

Instructions

Mix together the salt, lime juice, onion, pepper, tomatoes, and tomatillos. Spray you cooker with nonstick spray. Place ingredients in the following layers: quinoa, cheese, and squash, and top with more cheese. Place the tomatillo mixture over everything. Don't stir everything together. Set to slow cooker for 4 hours on low. Top with more cheese and oregano.

- *6 servings*

Spaghetti

A new, easy, and delicious way to make an Italian classic

Ingredients

- 3 oz parmesan
- 4 oz fontina cheese
- 1 tbsp oil
- package shredded mozzarella
- package shred cheddar
- 24 oz jar fire roasted tomato sauce
- 2 tsp garlic, minced
- 8 oz container onion/pepper mix
- 1 lb Italian sausage
- 8 oz spaghetti

Instructions

Brown the garlic, pepper mix, and sausage in a skillet. Mix everything in the cooker. Set to slow cook for 3 hours on low. Top with extra cheese.

- *6 servings*

Wild Mushroom Alfredo

Another vegetarian friendly dish that is full of flavor and protein.

Ingredients

- 4 c baby spinach
- pepper
- 1 c walnut halves
- 4 c grape tomatoes
- 1 c parmesan
- 9 oz wild mushroom agnolotti pasta
- 15 oz alfredo sauce

Instructions

Place some alfredo sauce in the cooker. Layer with one package of pasta, ½ cup parmesan, 2 cup tomatoes, and walnuts. Season with pepper and continue layering until ingredients are gone. Cover with alfredo sauce. Set to slow cook for 2 hours on high.

♦ *4 servings*

Wild Rice with Corn

A delicious dish that could be served as a main course or a side dish. Also, vegan friendly.

Ingredients

♦ 1/3 c basil
♦ ¾ c pecans
♦ 2 ¼ c boiling water
♦ ½ tsp salt
♦ ¾ c corn
♦ 1 ½ c onion, chopped
♦ ¾ c wild rice
♦ 2 ½ c sweet peppers, chopped
♦ nonstick spray
♦ 2 garlic cloves, minced
♦ 2 tsp oil

Instructions

Cook the garlic and the onions in a skillet until tender. Spray the cooker with nonstick spray. Place in the salt, corn, rice, peppers, and onion mixture. Mix together with the boiling water. Set to slow cook for 4 hours on low.

♦ *6 servings*

Fisherman's Wharf Seafood

This is a delicious dish full of delectable seafood and flavor.

Ingredients

- 2 tbsp parsley, chopped
- ¼ tsp hot sauce
- 1 c dry white wine
- ½ tsp salt
- 2 tbsp oil
- 1 tsp basil
- ½ lb shrimp, cleaned
- 1 lb tilapia, diced
- 1 tsp sugar
- 1 bottle clam juice
- bay leaf
- ½ tsp fennel seed
- 2 garlic cloves, chopped
- ½ c green bell pepper, chopped
- 3 c Italian plum tomatoes, quartered
- 1 c baby carrots, sliced
- 1 c leek, sliced

Instructions

In your cooker mix together the garlic, leek, and oil. Place in the clam juice, wine, bay leaf, fennel, pepper, tomatoes, and carrots. Mix well. Set to slow cook on low, eight to nine. Mix in the hot sauce, salt, basil, sugar, shrimp, and tilapia. Change temp to high and cook 20 minutes. Take out the bay leaf

- *8 servings*

Lemon and Herb Cod

A simple fish dish packed with flavor.

Ingredients

- lemons
- ¼ c water
- ½ lemon, juiced
- 2 tbsp herbs de provence
- 4 cod fillets

Instructions

Place the water in your cooker. Lay the fish in the pot. Season with the lemon juice and herbs de provence, and pepper and salt. Set to slow cook for 2 hours on low.

- *4 servings*

Paella

A quick dish that is full of flavor. With seafood and chicken, there is no shortage of meat.

Ingredients

- lemon wedge
- 1 ½ tsp garlic salt
- 1 tsp turmeric
- 1 ½ c long grain brown rice
- 1 bell pepper, chopped
- 1 ½ c diced tomatoes
- ½ tsp paprika
- 1 onion, chopped
- 1 ½ c vegetable broth
- 1 lb seafood medley
- 1 c peas
- 3 oz chicken sausage

Instructions

Brown the sausage in a skillet for a few minutes. Place the spices, salt, broth, tomatoes, pepper, onion, rice, and chicken and mix in the cooker. Set to slow cook. Let cook three hours on high. Stir everything again. Add in the seafood mixture. Cook for 30 minutes on high. Serve with lemon wedge.

- *8 servings*

Shrimp and Grits

A southern classic that is full of flavor and heat.

Ingredients

- siracha
- salt
- 3 tbsp butter
- ½ c mozzarella
- ½ c cheddar
- 1 tbsp chili seasoning
- ¾ c pepper onion blend
- 2 garlic cloves, minced
- 10 oz raw shrimp, cleaned
- 2 andouilla sausage, chopped
- 4.5 c water
- 1 vegetable bouillon cube
- 1.5 c grits

Instructions

Put the sausage, water, bouillon, and grits in the cooker. Set to slow cook 4-5 hours on low. Place the remaining ingredients in the pot, and cook 2 more hours. Serve with siracha.

6 servings

Vegetable Curry

These spicy vegetables are perfect for a vegan main dish. It's full of flavor that the whole house will love.

Ingredients

- 1 c peas
- 8 oz green beans
- 1 lg red bell pepper, sliced
- 8 oz cauliflower florets
- 2 onions, sliced
- 2 potatoes, chunked
- ½ tsp salt
- 2 ½ tbsp curry paste
- ¼ c AP flour
- 14 oz coconut milk

Instructions

Mix together the salt, curry paste, flour, and milk in your cooker until smooth. Mix in the pepper, cauliflower, onions, and potatoes. Pour the beans over top of everything. Set to slow cook for 6-8hours on low. The veggies should be tender. Mix in the cilantro and peas.

10 servings

Vegetarian Lasagna

Another great vegetarian dish that is just as flavorful as its full meat twin. People will be begging for more.

Ingredients

- 3 c mozzarella, divided
- 28 oz crushed tomatoes
- 15 lasagna noodles, uncooked
- pinch crushed red pepper
- 1 zucchini, quartered
- 3 large Portobello mushroom caps
- 5 oz package baby spinach
- 28 oz can diced tomato
- 3 garlic cloves, minced
- 15 oz container ricotta
- egg

Instructions

Mix together the zucchini, mushrooms, spinach, ricotta, and egg. Mix together red pepper, garlic, and both tomatoes in a separate bowl. Coat your cooker with nonstick spray. Put 1 ½ cups of tomato in the pot. Place noodles on top. Spoon in the veggie mixture. Place 1 ½ cup of sauce and sprinkle with mozzarella. Start another layer with noodles. Continue until you run out of ingredients. It should end with the tomato sauce. Set to slow cook. Let cook on high, two hours. Top with remaining mozzarella. Let the cheese melt for 10 minutes.

10 servings

Turkey Legs

This is a delicious game night food. It's full of flavor and juiciness, and it's fast to fix.

Ingredients

- 6 12 by 16 inch foil squares
- pepper
- salt
- 3 tsp poultry seasoning, divided
- 6 turkey legs

Instructions

Clean off the legs and dry. Season the legs with pepper, salt, and ½ tsp of poultry seasoning. Wrap each leg with foil when seasoned. Put the legs in the cooker with nothing else. Set to slow cook for 7-8 hours on low.

6 servings

Lamb Ribs

Everybody is familiar with pork and beef ribs, but not many know the goodness that is lamb ribs. This recipe gives you just that.

Ingredients

- 1 tsp EVOO
- pepper
- salt
- sprinkle thyme
- 5 garlic cloves, minced
- 1 lb lamb spare ribs

Instructions

Place the ribs in the pot. Place the other ingredients on top. Set to slow cook on high for one to two hours. Turn heat down to low and 8 more hours.

- *6 servings*

Teriyaki Short Ribs

Short ribs can be flavored in millions of different ways, and this is just another tasty option. The Instant Pot makes it quick and easy to do.

Ingredients

- 2 thai firecracker peppers, chopped
- 2 bunch green onions
- piece ginger, peeled and crushed
- 2 crushed garlic clove
- 2 small orange, halved
- ½ c packed brown sugar
- 1 c water
- 4 large beef short ribs
- ¾ c soy sauce

Instructions

Mix sugar, water, and soy sauce. Mix in orange juice. Slice up orange and place in sauce. Mix in onion, pepper, ginger, and garlic. Marinate the ribs in the mixture. Set to sauté, and heat oil. Add ribs and sear on both sides. Add marinade. Seal lid, and pick meat/stew. Cook 30 minutes.

♦ *4 servings*

Chops and Cabbage

This recipe provides you with your main dish and your side dish all in one. This spicy and sweet dish is sure to be a crowd pleaser.

Ingredients

- 4 thick pork chops
- 1 tsp pepper
- 2 tsp flour
- 1 tsp salt
- 1 tsp fennel seeds
- ¾ cup beef stock
- 1 tbsp oil
- medium cabbage head

Instructions

Set the pot to sauté. Season the pork with pepper, salt, and fennel. Slice cabbage into ¾ inch slices. Add the oil to the pot and brown the pork chops on one side. Take out the pork and place the cabbage in the pot. Put the pork on top of the cabbage with browned side up. Place the stock in the pot. Seal the lid in place. Set to high and cook, eight minutes. Let pressure release and take out the pork and cabbage. Set to sauté and let juices boil. Mix in the flour. Serve the cabbage and pork with the gravy.

♦ *4 servings*

Beef Back Ribs

Ribs are summer staple, but sometimes you want them when it's not grill weather. This recipe allows you to have them whenever you want.

Ingredients

- beef back rib rack
- 2 tsp fish sauce
- dry rub of your choice
- 4 tbsp coconut aminos
- salt
- 8 oz unsweetened applesauce
- 1 ½ cup water

Instructions

Clean and season the ribs with your choice of dry seasoning and salt. Cover and allow them to marinate for a few hours up to a day. Heat your broiler. Cut the rack of ribs apart so that they can fit in the pot. Lay them out on a cookie sheet a broil for a few minutes each side.

Mix the aminos, fish sauce, water, and applesauce together in the pot. Put a rack in the pot. Place the ribs in the pot on the rack. Set to high and cook for 20 minutes. Release the pressure. Take out the ribs and rack.

Set the pot to sauté and let the liquid begin to simmer. Allow the liquid to reduce for 5 minutes. Skim any fat off the top. Coat the ribs in the liquid and broil for a few more minutes.

♦ *4 servings*

Soups

Mushroom Marsala Soup

This soup is rich and creamy, which each component adding another layer to the flavor. Its savory warmth comes from the fresh rosemary and Marsala wine, while the mushroom provides a hearty base. You can serve this as a meal with some crusty bread or enjoy as a starter to your meal.

Ingredients

- 1 pound baby Portabella mushrooms (chopped)
- 4 cups chicken stock
- 2 tablespoons + 2 tablespoons butter
- 2 cups heavy whipping cream
- 2 tablespoons flour
- 1/2 cup dry Marsala wine
- 2 teaspoons fresh thyme (finely chopped)
- 1 cup onion (diced)
- 2 teaspoons fresh rosemary (finely chopped)
- 2 cloves garlic (chopped)
- Pinch of ground black pepper

Instructions

Use the sauté function of the cooker to melt 2 tablespoons of butter. Add the salt and onion and cook for two minutes. Then, add the mushrooms, fresh garlic, and black pepper, continuing to sauté until the mushrooms start to lose moisture. Add the wine and sauté for an additional two minutes. Then, add the chicken stock and fresh herbs to the pot. Cover the pot and cook this on high pressure for 3 minutes.

While you are waiting, add 2 tablespoons of butter to a sauté pan on the stove. Set this to a medium-high temperature until melted and then whisk in the flour, a little at a time. Cook for one minute and then take off the stove, setting the pan aside.

Use a quick pressure release once your cooker is done. Remove the lid and set the Instant Pot to sauté, letting the mixture inside come to a boil. Then, add in the mixture you prepared on the stovetop and mix well to combine.

Use an immersion blender to break up the mushroom pieces in the pot. If you do not have an immersion blender, you can put it into countertop blender. Once it is well blended, stir in the cream. If you would like, you can garnish with fresh pieces of Portabella mushroom, chopped parsley, or grated Parmesan.

♦ *4 servings*

Apple Parsnip Soup

This delicious soup is a warm and cozy addition to any winter evening. The freshness of the apple adds a crispness to the soup.

Ingredients

- ½ tsp salt
- 3 cans chicken broth
- 1 onion, chopped
- 2 apples, peeled and quartered
- 6 parsnips, peeled and chunked

Instructions

Place everything in the pot. Combine well. Close lid and set to slow cook. Set for 10-12 hours on low. Parsnips should be tender. Let it cool for 10 minutes. Place in a blender, and blend until smooth.

♦ *8 servings*

Black Bean Chili

This tasty chili is packed full of flavor and will warm of your insides. The hint of cocoa adds an additional flavor layer.

Ingredients

- ¼ tsp pepper
- 1 tbsp chili powder
- 2 garlic cloves, chopped
- 1 bunch scallions, chopped
- 1 c corn
- 1 tsp cocoa powder
- 1 tsp cumin
- 2 cans diced tomatoes with chiles
- ½ tsp salt
- 2 cans black beans

Instructions

Mix everything in the pot. Set to slow cook to high for 3-4 hours. You can serve the chili with sour cream, tortilla chips and cilantro.

♦ *10 servings*

Chicken Chowder

This thick chowder gives you a chowder besides corn. With the addition of chicken, you get lots of flavor and meatiness.

Ingredients

- ½ c half and half
- 2 carrots, chopped
- 1 tsp dill
- 1 small onion, chopped
- 2 c frozen corn
- 2 tbsp butter
- 2 cans cream of potato soup
- 1 ½ lbs chicken, diced
- 2 celery stalks, chopped
- 1 ½ c chicken broth

Instructions

Place everything in the cooker, except half and half, and stir to mix well. Set to slow cook for 3-4 hours on low. Chicken shouldn't be pink and veggies should be soft. Once done, mix in the half and half.

- *12 servings*

Chicken Dumpling Soup

This is a new take on chicken and dumplings, and makes it simple and easy to fix.

Ingredients

- ½ c 1 % milk
- 1 lb boneless chicken breasts, diced
- 1 ½ c biscuit mix
- 1 onion, chopped
- 10 oz frozen vegetables
- 2 cans chicken broth

Instruction

Put the onion, veggies, broth, and chicken in the cooker and mix well. Set to slow cook. Set time to five hours on low. Mix together the milk and biscuit mix. Drop spoonfuls into the soup. Cook for another hour on high. Season with some pepper.

♦ *6 servings*

Rosemary Chicken Noodle Soup

The rosemary in this soups adds a mature flavor to what is, typically, a kids soup.

Ingredients

- 3 ½ c egg noodles, uncooked
- ½ tsp pepper
- 4 c chicken broth
- 1 tsp salt
- ¼ c lemon juice
- 1 package baby spinach
- 1/3 c parsley, chopped
- 2 c onion, chopped
- 6 c water
- 1 package mushrooms, sliced
- 1 package carrot, shredded
- 1 tbsp rosemary, chopped
- 1 c celery, chopped
- 1 ½ lb boneless chicken breast, diced
- 1 ½ lb boneless chicken thighs, diced
- 1 tbsp olive oil, divided

Instructions

Place everything in the cooker and combine. Set to slow cook for 8 hours on low.

Enchilada Soup with Chicken

If you want a hot, flavorful dinner that is incredibly simple to make and is ready in 30 minutes, this is an excellent choice. You just open a few cans and throw some chicken breasts into your Instant Pot and you will have a tasty meal in about 30 minutes. You can add some personalization with toppings like tortilla strips, avocado, cheese, cilantro, or sour cream.

Ingredients

- 2 boneless skinless chicken breasts
- 2 cans black beans (drain and rinse)
- 1 28-ounce can enchilada sauce (mild)
- 1 14.5-ounce can diced tomatoes
- 2 cups frozen corn
- 2 cups chicken broth
- 1 4.5-ounce can mild green chilies (chopped)

Instructions

Add the enchilada sauce, chicken broth, tomatoes, and chili peppers to the Instant Pot and mix to combine. Add the chicken breasts and cook on high pressure for 5 minutes. When the timer goes off, wait for ten minutes and then use a quick pressure release.

Take the chicken breasts from the pot and shred. Return it to the pot and add the drained corn and black beans, stirring to combine. Use the simmer setting to bring the soup to a boil, stirring until the corn and beans are heated through. Top with your desired toppings and enjoy.

◆ *Makes 8 servings*

Creamy Chicken and Rice Soup

This hearty soup is perfect to enjoy for lunch or dinner on a cold day. Serve with a side of crusty bread or crackers or put in a bread bowl for an extra filling meal.

Ingredients

- 2 boneless skinless chicken breasts
- 4 cups chicken broth
- 6 ounces long grain wild rice
- 1 cup half and half
- 4 ounces cream cheese (cubed)
- 1 cup onion (chopped)
- 1 cup milk
- 1 cup celery (diced)
- 2 tablespoons butter
- 1 teaspoon salt
- 1 tablespoon dried parsley
- 2 tablespoons water
- 2 tablespoons cornstarch
- 1 cup carrots (diced)
- Dash of red pepper flakes
- ½ teaspoon black pepper

Instructions

Put your Instant Pot on the sauté setting and add the butter. Add the celery, carrot, and onion when the butter has melted and cook about 5 minutes, until the vegetables are tender. Then, add the wild rice, chicken, chicken stock, and spices to the pressure cooker. Cook for 5 minutes on high pressure. When the timer goes off, wait five minutes and then use a quick pressure release to get the lid off.

Take the water and cornstarch and mix them in a small bowl, until the cornstarch as dissolved completely. Set the pot on the sauté setting again and stir in the cornstarch. Add the cream cheese and stir continuously until it has melted completely.

Then, add the half and half and milk and cook until all of the ingredients are warmed, being careful not to bring the soup to a boil.

♦ *6 servings*

Chicken Noodle Soup

This every child's favorite soup, especially when they're sick. This is a quick and simple version of an American classic.

Ingredients

- 1 bag kluski noodles
- pepper
- ½ lb carrots, sliced
- 1 tbsp chicken bouillon
- 6 c water
- ½ onion, chopped
- salt
- 2 small potato
- 2 celery stalk
- 2 chicken breast

Instructions

Add onion, potato, celery, carrot, and chicken to pot. Pour in the water and bouillon. Seal lid. Set to soup for 40 minutes. Carefully release pressure. Remove chicken and shred. Place chicken back into soup mix. Sprinkle with pepper and salt.

♦ *8 servings*

Taco Soup

This tex-mex soup will comfort you on those long winter nights. It's tasty and everybody will love it.

Ingredients

- 1 c water
- 1 can black beans
- 1 can pinto beans
- 5 oz diced tomatoes with chiles
- 8 oz diced tomatoes
- 8 oz corn
- 1 tbsp taco seasoning
- ½ oz ranch dressing mix
- ¼ tsp pepper
- ½ tsp salt
- 2/3 c onion, diced
- 1 ½ c ground beef, cooked

Instructions

Add everything into the pot. Seal lid. Set to soup for 10 minutes. Carefully release pressure.

♦ *4 servings*

Chicken Taco Soup

Here is another flavorful soup. This is comfort food at its best. With a little spice, nobody can resist this soup.

Ingredients

- 8 oz tomato sauce
- 16oz chili beans
- 1 c diced onion
- 20 oz drained diced tomatoes with green chiles
- 1 ½ oz taco seasoning
- 4 c diced chicken
- 16 oz rinsed black beans

Instructions

Pour everything in the pot. Seal lid. Set to soup for 10 minutes. Carefully release pressure.

- *6 servings*

Butternut Squash Soup

This soup uses many mature flavors that most other soups lack. This a great choice for a date night appetizer.

Ingredients

- toasted pumpkin seeds
- salt
- olive oil
- 2 c stock
- ¼ tsp nutmeg
- pepper
- ¼ -inch ginger, peeled and sliced
- 1 small onion, chopped
- sprig sage
- 2 c cooked butternut squash

Instructions

Cook squash according recipe in side dish chapter. Set pot to sauté and cook onion, sage, pepper, and salt, until soft. Add squash and brown, about 10 minutes. Add stock, ginger, and nutmeg. Seal lid. Set to high for five minutes. Release pressure. Take out sage. With immersion blender, puree everything together. Garnish with pumpkin seeds.

- *4 servings*

Turkish Soup

This new take on a winter classic adds lots of flavor. You can adjust the flavor each time you make it by changing out the veggies that you use.

Ingredients

- ◆ salt
- ◆ 1 stalk coriander
- ◆ 1 onion, chopped
- ◆ 1 carrot, chopped
- ◆ ½ tsp paprika
- ◆ ½ tbsp rice
- ◆ 3 tsp olive oil
- ◆ 3 garlic cloves
- ◆ ½ c chopped vegetables, your choice
- ◆ 1 potato, chopped
- ◆ 1 c red lentils

Instructions

Set to sauté, and add oil and garlic. Cook to fragrant. Add everything else into the pot and 2 ½ c water. Lock lid, cook on high 9 minutes. Quick release pressure.

◆ *4 servings*

Chicken Soup

This is another version of the children's favorite. This one keeps it simple and focuses completely on the chicken.

Ingredients

- salt
- 4 c water
- 2 large carrot, chopped
- 2 small onion, diced
- pepper
- 4 diced potatoes
- 2 boneless chicken breast

Instructions

Place all ingredients in pot. Set pot to manual, 35 minutes. Once finished, release pressure naturally, 15 minutes, then quick release.

- *6 servings*

Cream Cheese Chicken

This creamy chicken soup brings lots of flavor to the table. It's quick and easy to make with minimal ingredients.

Ingredients

- 1 lb chicken
- ½ oz Italian dressing dry mix
- 4 oz cream cheese
- 5 oz cream of chicken soup

Instructions

Place everything in the pot. Seal lid. Set to poultry and cook for 15 minutes. Carefully release the pressure.

- *4 servings*

Chicken Curry

This chicken dish has lots of flavor and spice. The vegetables adds great texture and okra helps to thicken the soup.

Ingredients

- 6 oz chopped chicken breast
- 6 oz frozen okra
- 12 oz frozen veggie mix
- 1 tsp ground ginger
- 1/3 brick of golden curry sauce mix
- 3 cans water
- 1 can coconut milk

Instructions

Put everything in pot. Set to soup. Stir once finished cooking.

- *4 servings*

Chile Verde

This stew only takes two ingredients and it's full of flavor. This is great served over rice or on its own.

Ingredients

- 2 c green salsa
- 2 lb pork, chunked

Instructions

Set to sauté. Brown pork. Add salsa.Set to meat/stew, and cook 25 minutes. Shred pork.

♦ *6 servings*

Roots Chili

This chili is full of flavor and ingredients. All of the veggies pack in nutrients that everybody needs.

Ingredients

- 2 tbsp ACV
- 20 fl oz Beef broth
- 1 tsp cinnamon
- 16 oz pumpkin
- 4 tsp basil
- 2 c sweet potato
- 2 c carrot
- 1 ¼ c ground beef, cooked
- 1 ¼ tsp salt
- 1 ¼ tsp rosemary
- 16 oz sliced beets

Instructions

Blend beets in processor until smooth. Place all ingredients into pot. Seal and lock lid. Set to soup for 10 minutes. Carefully release pressure.

- *8 servings*

Cheddar Potato Soup

This is a hearty soup that will warm the soul any time of the year. The bacon and cheese add so many flavors to this dish.

Ingredients

- 4 tbsp bacon
- 4 tbsp cheese
- 1 tbsp salt
- 16 oz cream cheese
- 8 c chicken broth
- 10 tsp minced garlic
- 1 1/3 c onion, diced
- 5 c potato

Instructions

To the pot add, stock, seasonings, garlic, onion, and potatoes. Seal lid. Set to soup for 10 minutes. Quick release and turn off. Set to sauté. Mix in cream cheese. Mix until well combined. Top with bacon and cheese.

- *6 servings*

Red Borscht Soup

This fun soup is full of flavor and color. It is a fun dish that even children will love to eat.

Ingredients

- Squeeze ketchup
- 1 tsp sugar
- pepper
- 1 small onion, chopped
- beef stock
- 1 tsp red wine vinegar
- 2 red potatoes, cubed
- ½ c sauerkraut
- salt
- dill
- 1 clove garlic, minced
- oil
- 1 large beet

Instructions

Put beet on steamer rack. Pour in 1 ½ c water. Lock lid and cook on high, 30 minutes. Remove beet and cool in water. Peel, clean, and dice. Clean out pot.

Set to sauté and add oil. Sauté parsley, onions, salt, dill, and pepper until fragrant. Add beets, potatoes, tomatoes, sauerkraut, carrot, and garlic. Add as much broth as you like for desired consistency. Add sugar, ketchup, and vinegar. Adjust the taste. Cook on high, 10 minutes. Release pressure.

Serve with sour cream and parsley.

- *4 servings*

Potato Soup

This healthy and delicious dish will fill you up on those cold winter nights. The veggies will leave you feeling happy and healthy.

Ingredients

- ½ tsp salt
- ¼ tsp paprika
- 1 c broth
- 1 tbsp ground flax
- 1 c onion
- ½ c spinach, chopped
- ½ c celery
- ¼ tsp crushed red pepper
- 18-oz can roasted garlic starters
- ¾ c baby carrots, sliced
- 2 lb potatoes

Instructions

Put everything in pot and mix. Lock lid, set to soup and cook 30 minutes. Quick pressure release. Blend slightly with immersion blender. Adjust salt as needed. Top with cheese.

- *8 servings*

Homemade Tomato Basil Parmesan Soup

This creamy tomato soup is definitely not what you get in the can. It has a rich texture and accents of basil and Parmesan really bring out the sweetness of the soup.

Ingredients

- 3 pounds tomatoes (core, peel, and cut into quarters)
- 3 cans chicken broth
- 2 celery stalks (diced)
- 3 tablespoons butter
- 1 onion (diced)
- 1 carrot (diced)
- ½ cup shredded fresh Parmesan cheese
- 2 garlic cloves (minced)
- ¼ cup fresh basil
- ½ teaspoon salt
- 1 tablespoon tomato paste
- 1 cup half and half
- ½ teaspoon pepper

Instructions

Add the butter to the pressure cooker and allow it to melt. Then, add the carrots, onions, and celery and cook five minutes, or until tender. Add the garlic to the pot and cook for 1 minute, stirring frequently until the garlic becomes fragrant. Add the tomatoes, tomato paste, chicken stock, basil, and salt and pepper and cook for 5 minutes on high pressure. Allow to sit with the cooker off for 5 minutes and then do a quick pressure release.

Use an immersion blender (or remove and put in another blender) to puree the mixture until it is smooth. Then, set the cooker on sauté and stir in the half and half and Parmesan. When it is heated all the way through, serve. You can garnish with additional basil or Parmesan if you choose.

- *8 servings*

Appetizers and Side Dishes

Copycat Cilantro Lime Rice

This is one of the leading copycat recipes for Chipotle. The cilantro and lime pair beautifully for a fresh flavor. You can use it to make a homemade burrito bowl or serve alongside your favorite Mexican food. The best part is it can be made in less time than it takes to drive to Chipotle (unless you live next door).

Ingredients

- 1 tablespoon fresh squeezed lime juice
- 1 teaspoon salt
- 1 cup white rice (long grain)
- 3 tablespoons fresh cilantro (chopped)
- 1 ¼ cups water
- 2 tablespoons vegetable oil

Instructions

Add the water, rice, and salt to the pressure cooker and stir to mix. Cook for 3 minutes on high pressure. Use a natural pressure release when the timer goes off for 7 minutes, using a quick pressure release to release the remaining pressure. Use a fork to fluff the rice.

In a separate bowl, add the lime juice, cilantro, and oil. Whisk it together and then add to the rice, tossing until well combined.

- *2 servings*

Khichdi Dal

This is an interesting rice recipe to serve on the side of any main dish. If you're in the mood for something new, this is for you.

Ingredients

- 2 c water
- 1 tsp balti seasoning
- 1 tbsp butter
- ¼ tsp salt
- 1 c khichdi mix

Instructions

Rinse Khichdi. Set to sauté and melt butter. Add balti seasoning. Cook for a minute. Add Khichdi mix, water, and salt. Let boil and cover. Set to rice, 10 minutes. Release pressure. Fluff and serve.

- *4 servings*

Sweet Carrots

This is a great way to trick your children into eating their veggies. With a little bit of sugar your carrots are transformed to the next level.

Ingredients

- 4 c baby carrots
- ½ tsp salt
- 1 c water
- 2tbsp brown sugar
- 1 tbsp butter

Instructions

Pour water, salt, butter, and brown sugar. Set to sauté, and mix together. Add carrots and coat. Lock lid on. Set on steam, 15 minutes. Quick release the pressure. Take off lid. Set to sauté, and cook until liquid has evaporated.

- *4 servings*

Sweet Potatoes

Everybody loves having a sweet potato, but like a regular potato, they take forever to bake. With this recipe you will have one in less than 30 minutes. You can make as many or as little as you want.

Ingredients

- Sweet potatoes
- ½ c water
- olive oil

Instructions

Wash potatoes, rub with oil and cover with foil. Place water in pat and the trivet. Put potatoes in. Close and seal lid. Set for 15 minutes. Release pressure, and enjoy.

- *servings vary*

Coffee Can Bread

Most people probably don't think of cooking bread in their Instant Pot. This is a quick way to make homemade bread.

Ingredients

- 2 tbsp flour
- cooking spray
- coffee can
- personal bread recipes

Instructions

Fix your bread according to your recipe. Grease and flour the can. Roll bread in a ball and put it in the can. Cover with foil. Allow bread to rise. Place can in pot. Fill with water until it's ½ way up the can. Set on high for 15 minutes. Let bread cool, 10 minutes. Release pressure. Ease bread out of can.

♦ *servings vary*

Spaghetti Squash

This is a great starter to any healthy pasta dish. It's quick and easy, and a great alternative to pasta.

Ingredients

- 1 c water
- spaghetti squash

Instructions

Cut squash in half crosswise. Remove seeds. Place steamer in pot, add water. Place squash in pot. Cover and seal, cook on high 7 minutes. Quick release pressure. Remove and shred squash.

- *4 servings*

Garlic Potatoes

These are tasty potatoes that everybody will enjoy. They're a great addition to any dinner.

Ingredients

- 6 tbsp parsley
- salt
- ½ c milk
- 6 garlic cloves, chopped
- 1 c broth
- 4 medium russet potatoes

Instructions

Chunk potatoes. Put potato, broth, and garlic in pot. Lock lid and set to high, four minutes. Reduce pressure slowly. Mash potatoes, and add milk until you reach desired consistency. Sprinkle with parsley and salt.

◆ *4 servings*

Ricotta

Everybody seems to be making homemade cheese these days. This is a quick way to make ricotta.

Ingredients

- ♦ 3 c whey
- ♦ 3 c whole milk

Instructions

Set to yogurt. Pour in ingredients. Bring to boil. Add juice from a lemon and 1 tsp salt. Leave until clumps form. Strain with cheesecloth or drainer.

♦ *servings vary*

Basmati Rice

This is a quick way to make a perfect side dish to any meal. Rice seems to take forever to cook, but not in the Instant Pot.

Ingredients

- 2 c water
- 2 c Indian basmati rice

Instructions

Put everything in the pot and seal lid. Set to high for 6minutes. Quick release the pressure and fluff with a fork

- *4 servings*

Asparagus Risotto

This is a savory and sweet side dish that goes great with everything. It's also a great way to get your kids to eat their veggies.

Ingredients

- ½ c parmesan
- 2 tbsp thyme
- 1 c Arborio rice
- 2 small onion, chopped
- 4 tbsp orange juice
- 1 lb asparagus, cut ½-inpieces
- 2 tbsp olive oil
- 2 2/3 c vegetable stock
- 4 garlic cloves, chopped

Instructions

Clean and chop the asparagus. Set to sauté and heat oil. Add onion and until translucent. Mix in rice; stir well. Mix in garlic. Cook until fragrant. Pour in orange juice and stock, then lock the lid. Cook on high, 7 minutes. Release pressure. Carefully open and mix in thyme and asparagus. Cover with lid, and let it sit, five minutes. Pour into bowl and stir in parmesan.

♦ *4 servings*

Bavarian Cabbage

This recipes has an interesting take on cabbage. With the wine, apple, and cinnamon, this cabbage is going to be full of flavor.

Ingredients

- 2 tbsp AP flour
- 1 tbsp brown sugar
- 2 cinnamon stick
- 2small onion, diced
- ½ tsp ground cloves
- 2 bay leaf
- 2 tsp salt
- 1 c beef broth
- 1c dry red wine
- 4 tbsp wine vinegar
- 2 large apple, peeled and diced
- 2 tbsp butter
- 2 small red cabbage

Instructions

Slice up cabbage and remove core. Set to sauté, less. Melt butter. Add apple and onion until soft. Turn off. Add cabbage, wine vinegar, broth, red wine, salt, bay leaf, cinnamon, brown sugar, and cloves. Sprinkle with flour. Stir gently. Cook high, 8 minutes. Quick release. Turn off. Set to sauté, more. Boil, add cornstarch slurry. Thicken five minutes.

♦ *4 servings*

Fried Rice

This a tasty and crunchy side dish that's not just for Asian courses. It's full of flavor and veggies.

Ingredients

- 2 tbsp soy sauce
- 1 c matchstick carrots
- 4 tbsp sliced scallions
- 1 c diced ham
- 2 tbsp butter
- 3 c water
- 3 c brown rice

Instructions

Place everything in the pot and set to multi-grain. Fluff with a fork to finish.

- *4 servings*

Creamed Corn

Creamed corn is a southern staple, and this recipe makes it easier and tastier than ever.

Ingredients

- pepper
- 4-oz cream cheese
- 1 tsp sugar
- 2tbsp butter
- ½ c milk
- ½ tsp salt
- 1 lb corn kernels

Instructions

Mix the salt, corn, and sugar in pot. Pour in milk. Dot the top with cream cheese and butter. Lock lid in place and cook on high, 2 hours. Remove lid, and stir together. Adjust consistency, if needed, with a little milk. Add more salt or pepper if needed.

♦ *2 servings*

Braised Cabbage

This spicy side dish is not for the faint of heart. With red pepper flakes and cayenne it's sure to spice up your meal.

Ingredients

- 1 tsp cornstarch
- ¼ tsp red pepper flakes
- ¼ tsp cayenne
- ½ tsp sugar
- 2 tbsp ACV
- 2/3 c + 1 tsp water
- 1 small carrot, grated
- 1 small cabbage head, cut in 4 wedges
- sesame seed oil

Instructions

Set to sauté. Heat the oil, brown cabbage on a single side. Remove from pot. Add 2/3 c water, sugar, pepper flakes, vinegar, and cayenne. Add cabbage, seared side up, to the pot. Sprinkle with carrot. Lock lid, cook on high 5 minutes. Normal pressure release. Serve.

♦ *2 servings*

Mushrooms

This is a great start to a mushroom gravy, or if you want tasty mushrooms as a side dish.

Ingredients

- salt
- 6 tbsp soy sauce
- ½ c stock
- pepper
- 6 minced garlic cloves
- 1 onion, chopped
- 16 oz mushrooms

Instructions

Throw everything in the pot and seal the lid. Set to high for 4 minutes. Quick release the pressure. Set to sauté and let the sauce thicken.

- *4 servings*

Mexican Rice

This flavorful rice goes great with your favorite Mexican dish. The salsa and avocado adds an additional layer to the rice that you won't find other dishes.

Ingredients

- salt
- ½ c green salsa
- 2 ½ c broth
- 1 c cilantro
- pepper
- 1 avocado
- 2 c uncooked long-grain rice

Instructions

Mix broth and rice in cooker. Seal lid and cook on high 3 minutes. Once finished, let pressure release for ten minutes, then quick release. Fluff rice and cool slightly. Blend salsa, cilantro, and avocado until smooth. Stir mix into rice. Season with pepper and salt.

- *4 servings*

Cola Chicken Wings

This is the perfect game night wings for the person that doesn't like spicy. This Asian inspired wing dish is full of flavor and richness.

Ingredients

- 2 tbsp peanut oil
- 2tbsp rice wine
- 1 ½ c coca cola
- 2 tbsp ginger
- 2 stalk green onion
- 4 tbsp light soy sauce
- 2 tbsp dark soy sauce
- 8 crushed garlic cloves
- 3 lb chicken wings

Instructions

Set to sauté. Coat bottom with oil. Add onion, garlic, and ginger. Sauté until fragrant. Add wings and stir fry, two minutes. Mix in cola, and deglaze pot. Add in both soy sauces, and rice wine; mix. Lock lid, cook on high, 5 minutes. Turn off and release pressure.

- *8 servings*

BBQ Wings

Whether you are preparing for a party or want to have friends over for wing night, these wings are tender, crispy, and delicious. Use your favorite BBQ sauce to customize your finger-licking good wings.

Ingredients

- 2 pounds chicken drumettes and/or wings
- ½ cup BBQ sauce
- 1 cup cold tap water

Instructions

Add the water to the pressure cooker and then place a rack across the bottom. Arrange the chicken on the rack and close the lid. Cook for 5 minutes on high pressure and then use a natural release, which will take about 20 minutes.

While you are waiting, set the oven to 450 degrees so it can preheat. When the chicken drums and wings are done cooking, pat the wings dry. Throw them in a large mixing bowl and toss with the BBQ sauce. Then, layer them across a baking tray and wire rack. Bake for 8-15 minutes, until the sauce is caramelized and glossy.

- *2 servings*

Baked Potatoes

Everybody loves a bake potato, but they take so long to cook. These are done in a flash and you fix as many as you want.

Ingredients

♦ potatoes, however many you want

Instructions

Place the rack in the pot. Pour in a cup of water. Place the potatoes on the rack. Seal lid. Press manual and set time to 10 minutes. After finished, let the pressure release naturally.

♦ *servings vary*

Barley Cauliflower Risotto

This delicious side dish incorporates the flavor of sweet roasted cauliflower with barley risotto, which is a little chewier than traditional Arborio rice in risotto but the sauce it produces is incredible. Top with fresh grated Parmesan cheese if you would like. It tastes great as a side to pork or chicken.

Ingredients

♦ Small head of cauliflower
♦ 3 cups chicken broth
♦ 2 cloves garlic (minced)
♦ 2 sprigs thyme
♦ 1 cup pearl barley
♦ 2 tablespoons fresh parsley (chopped)
♦ 1 tablespoon butter
♦ 3 tablespoons olive oil, divided
♦ 1 large onion (diced)
♦ ½ cup fresh Parmesan (grated and divided)

Instructions

Start by roasting your cauliflower in the oven. Set the temperature to 425 degrees and allow your oven to preheat. Throw 2 tablespoons of olive oil in a Ziploc bag and season with salt and pepper to your taste. Set this to the side while you cover a baking sheet with aluminum foil. Take the cauliflower and spread it onto the tray.

Roast for 10 minutes once the oven is preheated. Then, toss the cauliflower and return it to the oven for an additional 10 minutes. During this time, heat 1 tablespoon of olive oil in the Instant Pot. Add the onion and cook on the sauté setting for about 5 minutes or until tender. Then, add the garlic and sauté until fragrant; about 1 more minute. Then, add the broth, barley, and thyme in the pressure cooker and cook for 25 minutes on high pressure. Use a quick release when finished and put on the sauté setting. Cook uncovered until the liquid reduces and the barley becomes tender. The "risotto" should now be thick and creamy. Remove the sprigs of thyme.

Once your cauliflower has cooked for 20 minutes, sprinkle with ¼ cup Parmesan cheese and return to the oven for 5 minutes. The cauliflower should be tender.

When the cauliflower is roasted and the risotto is finished, stir the cauliflower, the remaining Parmesan cheese, and the parsley and serve.

♦ *4 servings*

Savory Sweet Potato Mash

This mash is nothing like the sweet potato casserole that you traditionally eat around Thanksgiving. It is savory instead of purely sweet and takes only ten minutes to cook in the Instant Pot.

Ingredients

- 3 pounds sweet potatoes
- ¼ cup black pepper
- ½ teaspoon dried rosemary
- ¼ cup milk
- ½ teaspoon dried thyme
- 2 garlic cloves
- ½ cup fresh grated parmesan
- 2 tablespoons butter
- ½ teaspoon dried parsley
- ½ teaspoon dried sage
- 1 teaspoon salt

Instructions

Peel the sweet potatoes and chop roughly into pieces about 2 inches in size. Layer a rack across the pressure cooker. Set the potato pieces and garlic on top of it. Gently pour 1 ½ cups water into the cooker and cook them for 9 minutes on high pressure.

Do a quick release once these are done and drain the water. Use an electric mixer or potato masher to mash the garlic and potatoes. Then, add the remaining ingredients and stir until they are well combined. Garnish with additional fresh grated Parmesan if you would like.

♦ *6 servings*

Crispy Potatoes

These potatoes give you a fry like crunch without the added oil. Season the potatoes any way you would like, or keep them as the recipes tells you to.

Ingredients

- ½ lemon
- pepper
- ¼ c Italian parsley, minced
- salt
- 1 tbsp butter
- ½ lb fingerling potatoes, peeled

Instructions

Pour in ½ c water in the bottom of cooker and place in a steamer insert. Place potatoes in insert. Cover and seal with lid. Cook on high until high pressure has been reached. Lower to simmer and keep high pressure. Cook five minutes. Allow pressure to release.

Remove potatoes and water from cooker. Set to sauté and melt butter. Place in the potatoes and sprinkle with pepper and salt. Let them sauté for a few minutes, then flip and brown another minute. Squeeze the lemon juice over top and toss with parsley.

- *3 servings*

Israeli Couscous

Couscous has a wonderful texture that almost pops in your mouth. This is a great addition as a side to any meat or you can add a veggie and meat right in when it is finished to make a cooked meal.

Ingredients

- 2 cups couscous (Harvest Grain blend has lentils and red and green orzo)
- 2 ½ cups chicken broth
- 2 tablespoons butter

Instructions

Melt the butter using the sauté function on the Instant Pot. When warm, add the broth and couscous. Cook on high pressure for 5 minutes and use a quick pressure release. Use a fork to fluff and use salt and pepper to taste.

- *10 servings*

Butternut Squash

This recipe allows you to make whatever you want with you butternut squash. Nothing is added here, but that doesn't mean you can't get creative.

Ingredients

- butternut squash

Instructions

Place rack in pot and fill with 1 cup of water. Wash squash and cut if needed to fit in pot. Don't seed yet. Set on high for 15 minutes. When finished, quick release pressure. Open and cool about five minutes. Now cut the squash into fourths. Check to see how done your squash is.

If it's half way: cook another 15 minutes on high.

More than half: cook another 8 minutes on high.

Less than half: cook another 20 minutes on high.

It also depends on how you want to use the squash later on as to how soft you need it to be. Once done, quick release then fix as you please.

- *6 servings*

Acorn Squash

This healthy sweet dish will leave you begging for more. It's quick and simple to make and it can easily be frozen and reheated at a later date.

Ingredients

- Salt
- 1 tbsp brown sugar
- 1 tbsp butter
- ¼ c water
- 1 acorn squash, seeded and halved
- Pepper
- 1/8 tsp baking soda
- ¼ tsp ground nutmeg
- ½ tsp kosher salt

Instructions

Spread the salt and baking soda over the squash. Put the cooking rack in the pot and pour in ½ c water. Put the squash on the rack. Seal the lid and set to high. Cook for 20 minutes. Quick release and remove squash. Let squash cool.

Once you can handle the squash, scrape the inside into a bowl. Add nutmeg, butter, and brown sugar. Mash until the butter melts and squash is smooth. Taste to check the seasoning. Adjust as needed.

- *2 servings*

Sweet Brussel Sprouts

These are a sweet take on a vegetable that gets a bad rap. The orange juices and syrup adds a sweetness that even children won't be able to turn down.

Ingredients

- ♦ salt
- ♦ 2 tsp orange zest
- ♦ 1tbsp maple syrup
- ♦ 6 tbsp orange juice
- ♦ pepper
- ♦ 2 tbsp butter
- ♦ 1 lb brussel sprouts, trimmed

Instructions

Put everything in the pot. Seal lid in place. Set to four minutes for tender sprouts, or less if you want them crunchy. When finished, turn off and use quick release. Stir everything so that the sprouts are coated.

♦ *6 servings*

Stuffing

For this recipe, you will need a 6 cup Bundt pan that you can fit inside your pressure cooker. This results in a tender, flavorful stuffing that seems as if it has been cooked inside of a turkey or chicken for hours.

Ingredients

- 1 loaf bread (cubed and toasted in the oven)
- 1 ¼ cup chicken or turkey broth
- 1 medium onion (finely chopped)
- 1 cup celery (finely chopped)
- ½ cup butter
- 1 teaspoon poultry seasoning
- 1 teaspoon sage
- 2 teaspoons salt
- ¼ teaspoon pepper

Instructions

Put the Instant Pot on its simmer function and add the butter. When melted, add the onion, celery, and broth to the pot. Simmer about 6-7 minutes, until the celery and the onion are tender. Add the spices and mix well.

Put your toasted bread cubes in a bowl and add the prepared spice and veggie mixture over the top. Mix well, coating the stuffing as easily as possible. Use oil or cooking spray to coat the inside of your Bundt pan. Fill with the stuffing.

Prepare your Instant Pot by putting a rack inside. Use a 36" strip of foil to fold in half and layer beneath the Bundt pan, so you can remove it easily when finished cooking. Put the pan with the stuffing on top of this and cook for 15 minutes on high pressure. Use a quick pressure release.

Line a baking tray with foil and cooking spray while you are waiting. Preheat the oven to 350 degrees. Once the stuffing is finished, layer it on the pan and cook for 5-10 minutes to help the stuffing crisp a little.

- *10 servings*

Maple Bacon Squash

This sweet and healthy dish goes with anything. You can easily remove the bacon to make the dish vegetarian if you want.

Ingredients

- 1 tsp salt
- 2 tbsp maple syrup
- 4 lbs acorn squash
- 2 tbsp butter
- ½ c diced, cooked bacon

Instructions

Pour a cup of water, and add in the trivet. Lay the squash on the trivet. Seal the lid. Cook 8 minutes. Release pressure and let cool. Carefully take out the squash. Cut open and remove the seeds. Put the squash in pot. Seal lid. Cook for 8 more minutes. Release pressure. Allow to cool. Take out the squash. Scrape out flesh and mash with the maple syrup and butter. Mix in salt and bacon.

♦ *6 servings*

Refried Beans

This is a delicious side to goes great with almost any main dish. The spiciness can easily be adjusted by changing the amount of jalapeno you add.

Ingredients

- 3 c water
- ½ c salsa
- 1 tsp paprika
- ½ tsp black pepper
- 4 cloves chopped garlic
- 1 tsp cumin
- 1tsp chili powder
- 2 seeded jalapeno
- 2 medium onion, quartered
- 1 tsp salt
- 2 c dried pinto beans, rinsed

Instructions

Mix all ingredients in the instant pot. Seal the lid. Press manual and set time to 28 minutes. Once finish, allow to sit 10 minutes before releasing the pressure. Open, and stir.

Blend to the consistency that you would like with a blender, potato masher, or immersion blender. Be careful because the beans will be hot. If you want them to be thicker you can drain off some of the water as well.

- *6 servings*

Macaroni and Cheese

This is a perfect side, which all children love. This mac and cheese has a little bit of spice and whole lot of cheese.

Ingredients

- 6-oz shredded parmigiano
- 16-oz shredded sharp cheddar cheese
- 4 c water
- 1 tbsp salt
- 1 tsp hot sauce
- 2tbsp butter
- 1 lb macaroni
- 12-oz evaporated milk
- 1 tbsp mustard

Instructions

Mix together water, salt, hot sauce, mustard, butter, and macaroni in pot. Lock lid and cook on high, 4 minutes. Set to sauté. Stir in evaporated milk. Mix in cheese a handful at a time.

- *6 servings*

Snacks and Desserts

Rice Pudding

This delicious dessert is good hot or cold and you can take the raisins out if you do not like them. If you do refrigerate the pudding overnight, you may find that it becomes rather thick. If this happens, just stir in a little cold milk until it reaches your preferred consistency.

Ingredients

- 1 ½ cups water
- 2 eggs
- ½ teaspoon vanilla extract
- 1 cup Arborio rice
- ¼ teaspoon salt
- 1 ½ + ½ cup whole milk
- ¾ cup raisins
- ½ cup sugar

Instructions

Add the water, rice, and salt in the Instant Pot and cook for three minutes on high pressure. When it is finished, open with a natural pressure release. Do this for ten minutes and if any pressure remains, release it with a quick pressure release. Then, add the sugar and 1 ½ cups milk to the rice in the pot, stirring to mix.

Add the eggs, the remaining milk, and vanilla extract to a small bowl and whisk them together. Strain this through a mesh strainer into the pot. Turn the pot on sauté and stir constantly until you reach a boil. Turn off the Instant pot and remove the inner pan. Then, stir in the raisins. Serve warm or chilled. You may top with whipped cream, nutmeg, or cinnamon if you would like.

- *8 servings*

Crustless Lemony Cheesecake

A tart dessert that is perfect in the summer time.

Ingredients

- 1 c warm water
- 2 tsp lemon peel
- 3 eggs, beaten
- ½ tsp vanilla
- ½ c sour cream
- 1 tbsp AP flour
- 2 tbsp lemon juice
- ½ c sugar
- 12 oz cream cheese, softened
- nonstick spray

Instructions

Spray a soufflé dish with nonstick spray. Fix a foil sling under the dish. Mix together the vanilla, flour, lemon juice, sugar, and cream cheese. Mix in the sour cream and then the eggs. Fold in the lemon peel. Place batter in the dish. Cover with foil. Place the water in the cooker. Ease the dish into the cooker. Set to slow cook for 2 ¼ hours on high. Carefully remove the dish and let cool.

- *6 servings*

Peach Graham Cracker Upside Down Cake

This is a fun take on the upside down cake. Perfect summer dish when peaches are in season.

Ingredients

- ¼ tsp grated nutmeg
- ¼ tsp salt
- 2 tsp ginger, grated
- ½ c graham cracker, crushed
- 2 c AP flour
- ½ c butter
- 1 c milk
- 1 c brown sugar
- 1 egg
- ¼ c butter, softened
- 1 tsp baking soda
- ½ c brown sugar
- 3 peaches, sliced
- nonstick spray

Instructions

Cook your cooker with nonstick spray. Place peaches in bottom. Mix sugar, butter, and ginger in a pot and melt the sugar and butter. Place over top of the peaches. Mix the graham crackers and milk. Beat ½ cup butter and 1 cup brown sugar. Mix in the egg. Mix the flour, nutmeg, baking soda, and salt. Combine the wet, flour, and graham cracker mixture. Pour over the peaches. Set to slow cook for 2 ½ hours on high.

♦ *8 servings*

Peppermint Pretzel Candies

This is a fun holiday dessert that is great for a homemade gift that everybody will love.

Ingredients

- 3 oz dark chocolate, chopped
- ¾ c crushed peppermint
- 16 oz pretzel, chopped
- ½ tsp peppermint extract
- 3 tbsp butter
- 6 oz white caking chocolate, chopped
- 20 oz vanilla flavor candy coating, chopped

Instructions

Put a disposable liner in your cooker. Place in the butter, white chocolate, and candy coating. Mix well. Set to slow cook for 1 ½ hours on low. Stir often. Mix in the extract, peppermint candies, and pretzels. Place parchment paper on baking sheets. Place drops of the mixture on the baking sheets. Let stand until set. Milk the dark chocolate and drizzle over the candies.

- *4-8 servings*

Pumpkin Pomegranate Cheesecake

A quick and healthy cheesecake option. A perfect summer dessert when pomegranates are in season.

Ingredients

- ½ c pomegranate seeds
- 1 ½ tsp cornstarch
- ½ tsp vanilla
- ½ c pomegranate juice
- 1 tsp orange peel
- 3 eggs, beaten
- 2/3 c canned pumpkin
- 1 c warm water
- 1 tbsp brown sugar
- ½ tsp pumpkin pie spice
- 1 tbsp AP flour
- ½ c sugar
- 12 oz cream cheese, softened

Instructions

Mix everything together and pour into a prepared soufflé dish. Set to high for two hours.

♦ *6 servings*

Chunky Applesauce

This applesauce recipe is sweet, with just a hint of cinnamon. You can make it chunky as the recipe recommends or make it smooth by using an immersion blender or transferring it to a blender.

Ingredients

- 10 large apples (Jonagold)
- ¼ cup sugar
- ¼ cup water (or apple juice)
- 1 teaspoon cinnamon

Instructions

Peel and core your apples, then cut into slices. Add these to the pressure cooker with the other ingredients and mix together. Set the Instant pot for a cook time of 4 minutes on high pressure. When finished, use a quick release.

Take a spoon and break up the large chunks of apples until you reach the consistency you would like. You could alternatively use an immersion blender and blending until slightly chunky.

♦ *8 servings*

Cinnamon Poached Pears Topped with Chocolate Sauce

This simple dessert is a wonderful choice when pears are in season and the lovely shape of the pear makes for a great presentation. The pear is sweet and juicy, with cinnamon that accents its flavor and bitter chocolate syrup for a decadent touch. For ideal poached pears, choose a firm pair that is just ripe, as it begins to turn from green to its yellow color.

Ingredients

For the poached pears:

♦ 6 firm, ripe pears
♦ 3 cups water
♦ 2 cups white wine
♦ 1 lemon (halved)
♦ 2 cups cane sugar
♦ 6 cinnamon sticks

For the sauce:

♦ 9 ounces bittersweet dark chocolate (cut into ½-inch pieces)
♦ ¼ cup coconut oil
♦ ½ cup coconut milk
♦ 2 tablespoons honey

Instructions

Start by adding all of the ingredients for the poached pears except the lemon and the pears to pressure cooker. Put on the sauté setting and allow to simmer, continuing to stir until the sugar is completely dissolved. Then, put on the keep warm setting as you prepare the pears.

Pare the skin of the pears, keeping the pears whole and leaving the stems on. As soon as they are pared, rub the cut side of the lemon over them to prevent oxidization (the pears turning brown). Squeeze the leftover lemon juice into the pressure cooker and then drop the juiced lemon rind in as well. Add the pears to the syrup and cook for 3 minutes on high pressure, using a quick release when finished.

While you are waiting, you can make the chocolate sauce. Put the dark chocolate pieces into a bowl and set to the side. Use a medium flame to heat the coconut oil, maple syrup, and coconut milk to a boil. Pour this over the chocolate in the bowl and allow to sit while you remove the pears from the pan.

Use a slotted spoon to remove the pears and set on a plate. Allow the syrup to cool a bit and top the pears with it. Then, return to your chocolate. Whisk it together until smooth and keep warm until you are ready to serve you pears. When you are ready to serve, slice a small piece off the bottom of your pears so they stand straight up. Place one pear on each plate and top with the warmed chocolate.

♦   *4 servings*

Tapioca Pudding

This is a delicious dessert or snack that everybody will enjoy. It's simple and easy to make and stores well.

Ingredients

- 1 lemon, zested
- ½ c sugar
- ½ c water
- 1 ½ c whole milk
- 6 tbsp tapioca pearls

Instructions

Add a cup of water and steamer basket to cooker. Rinse tapioca. In a heat proof bowl, mix milk, lemon zest, tapioca, sugar, and milk until sugar dissolves. Ease the bowl into the cooker and seal lid. On high pressure, cook 8 minutes.

When finished, turn off cooker and let pressure release on its own. After pressure is released allow it to set another five minutes. Carefully remove bowl and stir with fork pouring into bowls. Cover and refrigerate three hours.

♦ *4 servings*

Chocolate Cake

This is a classic dessert, that's everybody's favorite. You can frost and decorate it however you please.

Ingredients

- ½ tsp vanilla
- ½ tsp lemon juice
- ¼ c milk
- ¼ c water
- 3 tbsp cocoa powder
- 1 egg
- ½ c sugar
- ¼ tsp salt
- 3 tbsp butter, softened
- ¾ tsp baking soda
- ¾ c flour

Instructions

Combine the baking soda, flour, and salt together. Mix together the butter and sugar in another bowl. Mix in the egg until fluffy. Whisk in the cocoa and water and mix until incorporated. Mix in lemon juice and vanilla. Mix in milk. Slowly fold in the flour mixture. Don't over mix. Grease 6 inch cake pan, and pour in batter.

Heat cooker with a plate or tray on bottom, close lid. No water, no gasket. Once it has heated for 2 minutes, gently place cake pan in the cooker with a pot holder. Close lid, and keep heat low. Cook 45 to 50 minutes. Cake will separate from the edges of the pan, and toothpick should come out clean. Let it for 10 minutes then turn out on platter. You can eat as is, or frost with your favorite frosting.

- *6 servings*

Key Lime Pie

This summer classic just became easier to fix. This is a great dessert to take to barbecues and get-togethers.

Ingredients

Crust:

- ♦ 1tbsp sugar
- ♦ 3tbsp butter, melted
- ♦ ¾ c graham-cracker crumbs

Filling:

- ♦ 2tbsp key lime zest
- ♦ 1/3 c sour cream
- ♦ 4 large yolks
- ♦ ½ c key lime juice
- ♦ 1 can sweetened condensed milk

Instructions

Coat 7-in springform with oil. Mix together the crumbs, butter, and sugar. Press into pan and freeze 10 minutes. Beat yolks until light. Beat in milk until thick, then add juice. Fold in zest and sour cream. Pour into crust. Cover with foil.

Fill pot with a cup water, and place in trivet. Place a foil sling around pan and place in pot. Seal lid. Cook on high for 15 minutes. Let pressure release for ten minutes, then release remaining pressure. Take out the pan and set on a cooling rack. Refrigerate 4 hours. Top with whipped cream.

♦ *6 servings*

Baked Apples

These are tasty, quick apples that make the perfect dessert. They are easy to store and travel with.

Ingredients

- 1 tsp cinnamon
- ½ c sugar
- ½ c red wine
- 6 tbsp raisins
- 4 apples, cored

Instructions

Place apples in cooker. Add cinnamon, sugar, raisins, and wine. Lock lid, cook on high 10 minutes. Natural release pressure. Ease apples out and serve with liquid.

♦ *4 servings*

Chocolate Fondue

This is a great date night food. Its perfect served with strawberries, bananas, or any other fruit.

Ingredients

- 3.5 oz fresh cream
- 3.5 oz bittersweet chocolate

Instructions

Add two cups water and trivet to pot. Add ingredients to a heat proof bowl. Place in cooker. Cook on high 2 minutes. Slowly release pressure. Ease out bowl. Stir chocolate mixture until it comes together.

- *2 servings*

Cranberry Bread Pudding

The dessert is popular around the holidays. Not only are cranberries delicious, but they add a holiday color.

Ingredients

- 3 tbsp chopped nuts
- whipped cream
- ¾ c water
- 3 tbsp dried cranberries
- 1.5 c dry bread cubes
- ½ tsp vanilla
- ¼ c sugar
- 1 c milk
- 2 eggs

Instructions

Grease a soufflé dish and criss cross two strips of foil on the bottom. Beat vanilla, sugar, milk, and eggs together. Put the cranberries and bread in prepared dish. Pour in the egg mixture and top with foil. Place 1 ½ cups water and trivet in the pot. With a foil sling, lower dish into pot. Lock and seal lid. Cook on high 25 minutes. Release pressure. Carefully life out dish. Serve topped with whipped cream.

♦ *10 servings*

Crème Brulee

Impress your friends by making this tasty French dessert. Typically looked at as a hard dessert to make, this recipe makes it easy.

Ingredients

- 6 tbsp superfine sugar
- 2 c heavy cream
- ¼ tsp salt
- 6 tbsp sugar
- 1 ½ tsp vanilla
- 8 egg yolks

Instructions

Add a cup and half of water to the pot and add the trivet. Mix together salt, sugar, and yolks. Mix in vanilla and cream until blended. Strain liquid into a pitcher. Pour into custard cups. Top each with foil. Set the cups on the trivet. Seal lid. Cook on high for 6 minutes. Carefully release pressure. Uncover and let cool. Wrap in saran wrap and place in the fridge to cool for 2 hours. When ready to eat, sprinkle on superfine sugar and brown with a blow torch.

- *4 servings*

Amaretti Stuffed Peaches

This crunchy and sweet dessert adds an extra layer to the classic poached peach. With the cookies, it's like two desserts in one.

Ingredients

- ♦ 2 peaches, firm
- ♦ 1 tsp lemon zest
- ♦ 2 tbsp butter, melted
- ♦ 2 tbsp almonds
- ♦ 1 c amaretti cookies, crumbled
- ♦ 4 tbsp sugar
- ♦ 1 c red wine

Instructions

Pour in sugar and wine and place in steamer basket. Mix almonds, cookies and zest together, and stir in melted butter. Clean the peaches. Slice in half and take out pit. Carve out the cavity a little more. Dust and fill the peaches with the cookie, and then ease into the pot. Seal the lid. Turn to high and cook for three minutes. Let pressure release and remove the peaches. Reduce the wine until it is a syrup consistency and drizzle over peaches.

♦ *2 servings*

Blueberry Pudding

This fresh summer pudding is great on a warm evening. It's simple to make and delicious to eat.

Ingredients

- ¼ lb blueberries
- 3.5 oz milk
- egg, beaten
- ¼ c sugar
- 1 ¼ tbsp breadcrumbs
- ¼ c butter
- ¼ tsp salt
- ¾ tsp baking powder
- ½ c flour

Instructions

Grease heat proof bowl. combine the salt, baking powder, and flour. Cut in butter. Add sugar and breadcrumbs. Stir in milk and eggs. Gently fold in blueberries. Fill bowl ¾ full. Make a foil sling. Heat a cup of water in cooker. Place in steamer rack. Place bowl in pot. Cover, but don't seal. Steam 15 minutes. Lock lid, cook high pressure 35 minutes. Quick release pressure. Ease out the bowl, and turn out on plate.

- *6 servings*

Pineapple Upside Down Cake

This is a fun cake and this recipe makes it easier and faster to make. It's perfect for a birthday or a holiday and everybody enjoys it.

Ingredients

- 2 eggs
- 1 c powdered sugar
- ¼ c milk
- 1 ½ c AP flour
- ½ c butter
- ½ tsp baking soda
- maraschino cherries
- 1 tsp baking powder
- 3 tbsp pineapple juice
- 6 slices pineapple
- 2 tbsp sugar
- 1 tsp butter

Instructions

Grease cake pan and sprinkle with 2 tbsp sugar. Arrange pineapple in pan, and place cherries in the centers. Beat eggs until they become fluffy. Mix in sugar and salt. Mix in oil, milk, and juice. Mix together the baking soda and powder, and flour. Slowly mix together dry and wet ingredients. Pour into prepared pan. Place rack in cooker, and heat for 10 minutes. Using foil sling, place cake in pot. Close lid, don't seal. Cook on medium 40 minutes. Check for doneness with a toothpick. Carefully remove cake and cool 30 minutes. Invert onto a plate.

♦ *8 servings*

Molten Chocolate Cake

This is a fun date night cake to have. When done perfectly, chocolate will ooze out of the center when cut into.

Ingredients

- ½ tsp baking powder
- pinch salt
- 1 tbsp cacao powder
- 4 tbsp AP flour
- 4 tbsp milk
- 4tbsp sugar
- 2 tbsp EVOO
- 1 egg

Instructions

Grease heat proof cups. Place trivet and a cup of water in the cooker. Mix everything together. Pour in cups. Put the cups in the pot, close and seal lid. Cook for 6 minutes. Carefully remove and sprinkle with sugar.

- *2 Servings*

Cheese Flan

This is a new take on the Mexican dessert, flan. It's easy to make, but it takes a lot of patients to allow it to set up in the fridge.

Ingredients

- 6 tbsp sugar
- dash cinnamon
- 1 tsp vanilla
- dash nutmeg
- 14-oz sweetened condensed milk
- 5 eggs
- 12-oz evaporated milk
- 8-oz cream cheese

Instructions

Set to sauté. Place flan pan in pot with sugar in bottom. Melt sugar in the pan. Stir until browned. Take out of pot. Mix cream cheese and eggs. Add rest of the ingredients. Pour in pan and cover. Pour a little water in pot, and put pan on trivet in pot. Cook on high, 15 minutes. Release pressure slowly. Refrigerate 7 hours. Turn out on plate.

- *6 servings*

Dulce De Leche

This is a delicious sweet treat that can be used as an ice cream topper, or eaten alone.

Ingredients

- 1 can sweetened condensed milk

Instructions

Place can in the bottom of the pot on its side. Fill with cold water to an inch above the can. Lock the lid. Heat to high pressure. Cook 40 minutes. Turn the pot off and let pressure release. Carefully take out the can. Open can, and enjoy.

- *Servings vary*

Pots de Crème

Another French dessert to impress people with. It's a fresh, rich dish that can be served all sorts of fruits.

Ingredients

- black berries
- ¾ c white sugar
- 1lemon
- 6egg yolks
- 1 c fresh cream
- 1 c whole milk

Instructions

Peel the lemon. Add lemon zest, milk, and cream to a sauce pan. On medium heat allow everything to come to a bubble. Set off heat and cool completely. Add the minimum amount of water to your pot. Whisk together the sugar and yolks. Pour slowly into the cream mixture. Make sure not to over mix. Pour through a strainer. Pour mixture into ramekins. Place foil over ramekins and sit in pot. Lock and seal lid. Set to high for 10 minutes. Release the pressure naturally. Carefully remove and let sit for 40 minutes. Serve with blackberries.

♦ *4 servings*

Peanut Butter Chocolate Cheesecake

This delicious dessert is made for individual servings. It's like a peanut butter cup in a jar that everybody will love.

Ingredients

♦ 2 tbsp sugar
♦ ¼ tsp vanilla
♦ ¾ tsp cocoa
♦ 1 ½ tsp powdered peanut butter
♦ 1 egg
♦ 4 oz cream cheese

Instructions

Ingredients should be room temp. Mix eggs and cream cheese until smooth. Mix in the remaining ingredients. Pour into two 8-oz mason jars, cover with foil. Add trivet and cup of water to pot. Put in pot and cook on high 16 minutes. Release pressure naturally. Chill for a couple of hours. Serve with whipped cream.

♦ *2 servings*

Red Wine Pears

This dessert will trick anybody into thinking it's gourmet, and only you will know the secret. It's deliciously easy.

Ingredients

- ½ c sugar
- piece of ginger
- cinnamon stick
- 1 clove
- ¼ bottle red wine, your choice
- 2 pears, peeled

Instructions

Pour wine in cooker. Add cinnamon, clove, sugar, and ginger, and mix. Add pears and lock lid. Cook on high for 6 minutes. Release pressure slowly. Carefully remove pears. Turn pot to sauté and reduce liquid. Drizzle over the pears.

♦ *2 servings*

Banana Polenta Porridge

This is a healthy take on banana pudding. It's a delicious and healthy dessert that everyone is sure to love.

Ingredients

- 1/8 c polenta
- ½ tsp vanilla
- 2 tbsp apple juice
- 1 ½ tbsp lemon juice
- 1/3 c rice
- 1 banana, chopped
- dash turmeric
- 1 c water
- 1 c milk

Instructions

Set pot to sauté. Place everything in pot except polenta. Bring to boil. Turn off then set to high for 5 minutes. Release pressure and whisk in polenta. Serve when thickened.

♦ *4 servings*

Pumpkin Brown Rice Pudding with Dates

Plump dates and sweet pumpkin makes this rice pudding a delicious fall dessert. The brown rice makes this both more filling and healthier than traditional rice pudding recipes.

Ingredients

- 3 cups cashew milk (or another dairy-free alternative)
- 1 cup brown rice (short grain)
- ½ cup pitted dates (chop into small pieces)
- 1 cup pumpkin puree
- ½ cup water
- ½ cup maple syrup
- 1 cinnamon stick
- 1 teaspoon vanilla extract
- 1 teaspoon pumpkin spice mix

Instructions

If you want your brown rice to be softer instead of chewy, put it in a bowl and cover it with boiling water for 10 minutes to an hour before you start cooking. Rinse when you are finished.

Use the simmer setting to bring the water and milk to a boil in your Instant Pot. Add the rice, cinnamon stick, dates, and salt. Cook on high pressure for 20 minutes and then use a natural press release, which will take about 20 minutes.

Then, stir in the pumpkin puree, pumpkin spice mix, and maple syrup. Stir constantly for 3-5 minutes while cooking on the sauté setting. This will cook out some of the pumpkin flavor to keep it from being overpowering and thicken the pudding. Turn off the pressure pot and remove and discard the cinnamon stick. Stir the vanilla into the mix.

Move the pumpkin pudding into a bowl and use plastic wrap to cover the surface, making sure that the wrap touches the surface of your pudding. This will stop a skin from forming and keep the surface from collecting condensed water from the steam. Allow to cool for about 30 minutes before serving. You will notice that this thickens the pudding even more. If you would like, you can top with cool whip or a sprinkle of cinnamon.

♦ *6 servings*

Chilled Fruit Soup

This delicious soup can be made with any seasonal fruits. It is like a smoothie but better because the cooking process really brings out the flavor of the fruit. You can add raspberries or strawberries to give it a pretty pink color or throw in whatever fruit you would like.

Ingredients

- ½ cantaloupe
- 2 peaches
- 1 large orange
- 2 cups pineapple juice
- 1 tablespoon Chia seeds
- 1 cup Greek yogurt (plain)
- 1 tablespoon powdered sugar
- ½ teaspoon vanilla extract

Instructions

Start by preparing the fruit. Remove the rind from the cantaloupe and cut it into chunks, remove the pits from the peaches and cut in half, and peel the orange and cut it in half. Add these fruits with the pineapple juice to your Instant Pot and cook for 5 minutes on high pressure. Do a quick pressure release when the timer goes off.

Take the mixture and pour it through a strainer into a large bowl, removing the remaining pulp. Allow the mixture to cool to room temperature and add the remaining ingredients, stirring to combine.

♦ *4 servings*

THE END

Conclusion

The Instant Pot pressure cooker is an incredibly fast, useful appliance that you can use to make any number of meals. It prepares tasty meals in no time at all. While the many buttons can be a little overwhelming at first, you will quickly learn how to use each and what each does as you start to cook delicious meals that you and your family will love.

There is nothing holding you back now. Try out some of the recipes in this book and once you are learning, make your own! The possibilities are really endless with the Instant Pot on your countertop.

Happy cooking!

Made in the USA
San Bernardino, CA
06 February 2017